CATHOLICS, MARRIAGE AND DIVORCE:
Real People, Real Questions

catholics, marriage and divorce:

REAL PEOPLE, REAL QUESTIONS

VICTORIA VONDENBERGER, R.S.M., J.C.L.
Tribunal Director
Archdiocese of Cincinnati

ST. ANTHONY MESSENGER PRESS

Cincinnati, Ohio

Nihil Obstat: Rev. David L. Zink
Donald Miller, O.F.M.

Imprimi Potest: Fred Link, O.F.M.
Provincial

Imprimatur: +Most Rev. Carl K. Moeddel, V.G.
Auxiliary Bishop
Archdiocese of Cincinnati
August 26, 2003

The *nihil obstat* and *imprimatur* are a declaration that a book or a pamphlet is considered to be free from doctrinal or moral error. It is not implied that those who have granted the *nihil obstat* and *imprimatur* agree with the contents, opinions or statements expressed.

The scriptural quotations are from the *New Revised Standard Version Bible,* copyright ©1989 by the Division of Christian Education of the National Council of Churches of Christ in the United States of America. Used by permission. All rights reserved.

Canons cited with permission from *Code of Canon Law, Latin-English Edition, New English Translation.* Washington: Canon Law Society of America, 1999. All rights reserved.

Cover and book design by Mark Sullivan

Library of Congress Cataloging-in-Publication Data

Vondenberger, Victoria.
Catholics, marriage, and divorce : real people, real questions /
Victoria Vondenberger.
p. cm.
Includes index.
ISBN 0-86716-514-6 (alk. paper)
1. Marriage–Religious aspects–Catholic Church. 2.
Divorce–Religious aspects–Catholic Church. 3. Pastoral
theology–Catholic Church. 4. Catholic Church–Doctrines. I. Title.
BX2250.V66 2003
262.9'4–dc22
2003022204

ISBN 0-86716-514-6
Copyright ©2004, Victoria Vondenberger
All Rights Reserved.
Published by St. Anthony Messenger Press
www.AmericanCatholic.org
Printed in the U.S.A.

Joe and Daisy Vondenberger
July 10, 1943

Dan and Sandy Vondenberger
February 17, 1979

DEDICATION

This book is dedicated to

two very special couples:

in memory of my parents,

Joe and Daisy Vondenberger,

whose marriage

was lifelong;

and in gratitude for my

brother Dan and his wife

Sandy, whose marriage so

enriches my life.

FOREWORD

This book is unique in several ways. One is that its table of contents was not written by the author, but by a whole group of anonymous questioners: users of the OnceCatholic.org Web site. It was they who determined what the author would have to write about. Secondly, one could contend that the material contained here was originally not written at all, if writing means putting marks on paper or stone. These answers were communicated via e-mail in response to questions that came via e-mail. They mirror the wonders of electronic communication (which many of us use and are grateful for, but which few of us really understand).

Yet in other ways, what is offered here is quite ordinary: questions that people have about marriage, about Catholic canon law, about the nature and demands of the sacraments. People have wanted to know things about all these matters, not just since the advent of e-mail, but arguably for as long as there have been rules and regulations governing the sacrament of matrimony, i.e., for as long as there has been a sacrament of matrimony.

Why? Why do people have so many questions about so many aspects of marriage? Basically it's because marriage is a complicated reality.

Most fundamentally, marriage involves God's plans for the personal union of men and women, for the way they would express their love for one another, for the way they would beget and bring up their children. It involves the specifically Christian view that this union of woman and man is meant to express the love of Christ for His Church. This is a love of self-giving, of permanence, a love that knows no other love, a love that is open to new life. Sacramental marriage, therefore, is meant to include lifetime commitment, total faithfulness to the spouse, and an openness to children. These are not values that are highly thought of in our culture. Hence, the theology of Christian marriage often looks complex and perhaps even quaint to people of our time and place. They have lots of questions about it.

Then there is the law of the Church. As the Church has reflected on the nature of marriage over the centuries, it has teased out of the theology of marriage many practical consequences: Who can contract a valid sacramental marriage? How old do you have to be? Where can the wedding take place? What specific formalities need to be observed? Most ordinary people are not well versed in these matters. That's why we have experts trained in the Church's law. But that doesn't mean that ordinary people can't or shouldn't have questions.

Then there is the fact that marriage is not just a religious event, but a civic one as well. Just as the Church has its rules about marriage, so does civil society. These rules need to be respected, too. They, too, raise questions.

Then there is the social aspect of marriage, the way other people observe and participate in this important undertaking in the lives of those they love. Who gets invited? In whose church will the wedding take place? What say should parents have in the details of the wedding?

And we haven't even mentioned yet the love of bride and groom for one another, their concerns, their wishes, their preferences.

All these things are important. Some are more important than others, but every aspect of marriage calls for attention. What's hard is to find a way to respect each facet of marriage without overlooking any of the others. Theology, canon law, civil law, social custom, personal taste: each has its part to play but it's not always easy to see how they all fit together. That's why people have questions about marriage.

Add to that that no two sets of personal circumstances are ever exactly the same. Just as individual human beings are one of a kind, so marriage situations and marriage questions tend to be one of a kind. True, there are unvarying principles that have to be followed in each marriage, but the specific details of this particular marriage make it different from practically every other marriage situation. That, too, contributes to the questions.

What is presented here is a series of answers to a series of particular questions about particular marriage situations. Many readers with questions of their own will not find a detailed answer to those questions here. But they will at least know that other people have questions, too. They will learn about the general outlines and issues that come into play in the questions. And, most important of all, they will learn that there are answers.

I believe that Sister Victoria and her Companions in the Marriage Room of the OnceCatholic.org Web site have done a great service to a great number of people by making their expertise available both electronically and now in book form. May the Lord bless them and may the Lord bless all those who have come with their questions. I hope that all the questioners are as grateful to the answerers as I am.

Most Rev. Daniel E. Pilarczyk
Archbishop of Cincinnati

INTRODUCTION

This book is based on the "Marriage Room" at
www.OnceCatholic.org, a Catholic Web site, which began on
Ash Wednesday, February 28, 2001. This Web site was
initiated by St. Anthony Messenger Press to reach out to
Catholics who are not practicing their faith. As the
publisher, Rev. Jeremy Harrington, O.F.M., noted in his letter
of November 1, 2000 to bishops of the Church, "Many
Catholics who do not practice their faith would never
identify themselves as anything other than as Catholics." The
site was created and designed to provide a personal
connection with someone in the Church, as well as
information about situations that may be keeping a person
from fully practicing the Catholic faith.

Archbishop Daniel E. Pilarczyk of Cincinnati, which is
the location of St. Anthony Messenger Press, offered his
support to this initiative. Archbishop Pilarczyk wrote that he
was delighted to hear about this Web site geared to
Catholics who felt they had been alienated by the Church.
He expected "that the Spirit will use this site to help people

return to the practice of their faith." The Archbishop encouraged priests and parish ministers throughout the Archdiocese of Cincinnati to make this site—with its access to a whole group of professional people available at no cost to local churches—known to their constituencies. My hope is that many other dioceses also take advantage of the resources this site has to offer.

The June 2002 issue of *St. Anthony Messenger* magazine reported that this site averages 900 user sessions a day. Within a year, there were so many visits to the Marriage Room that the publishers assigned a third Companion to help answer the hundreds of questions posed in the Marriage Room. In fact, there were so many questions in the Marriage Room that the Companions began editing it down at least once a month, combining questions and responses and eliminating duplicate items. As of June 2003, three thousand entries had been deleted.

According to *The Catholic Journalist* May/June 2002 edition, the Catholic Press Association (CPA) honored the OnceCatholic.org Web site with the *First Place Award for Best Web Site*. The CPA stated that the site has the "most visually stunning and professional design of all sites." They recognized the site for its eye-pleasing flash display as well as "excellent content, very personal, relatable and informative." Additionally, the CPA praised the site for using "on-line interactiveness" effectively, by responding to individual questions, while maintaining mass appeal (*Catholic Journalist*, 32).

That mass appeal and the very high volume of hits to the Marriage Room of the Web site led those in charge of the site, Rev. Patrick McCloskey, o.f.m and Rev. Gregory Friedman, o.f.m. to approach me (as the Director of the

Tribunal in Cincinnati) and ask if I would author this text based on the Marriage Room. In order to write the book, I approached the sister and two priests who are the Companions on the site and asked for their approval for the publishing of this book. They agreed to the publication of the questions and answers, as well as to my editing of the material in both their responses and the questions. They explained to me that part of their duties as Companions is to delete any specific references that would enable someone to identify a questioner, and I have tried to do that also. The Companions and I are also aware that all three Companions work in the United States and sometimes questions come from other countries where local procedures may differ from what has been established by the United States Catholic Conference of Bishops (USCCB). The Companions and I have tried to be conscious of that in the responses.

I offer this text with deep gratitude to the three Companions in the Marriage Room who have spent many hours taking turns responding each day to the questions of those who seek advice or reassurance. I am very grateful to Mary Cathleen Curran of St. Anthony Messenger Press for her capable assistance in organizing the material for this book as well as her most valuable non-canonist viewpoint about whether particular information was clearly presented. I also express my gratitude to the Franciscan Province of St. John the Baptist, which is headquartered in Cincinnati, Ohio, and is also the sponsor of St. Anthony Messenger Press and of this Web site. Additionally, I would like to extend great appreciation on behalf of the many people who have written to say how much this site has helped them.

I hope readers will find this book a very palatable way to obtain information about Church law and marriage. I also hope that readers will feel the reality of the questions posed since they actually come from people dealing with these issues in their own lives. The variety of questions, the complicated circumstances and the careful responses from the Companions make this book quite different from other books about Catholic marriage and marriage cases. Previous books on this topic offer a scholar's carefully prefabricated questions that invite very tidy responses. This book contains the messy stuff of real life. It offers stories and questions from real people. Juggling the precision needed to be canonically correct with the desire to be understood by ordinary readers, the Companions take time to offer heartfelt, well-researched information in ordinary language.

May our God bless you and those whose lives you touch,

Sister Victoria Vondenberger, R.S.M., J.C.L.

PART 1:

THINGS TO CONSIDER BEFORE MARRIAGE

IMAGINE FOR A MOMENT, A LAND LONG AGO AND FAR AWAY, where every young woman was born with a small birthmark in the shape of a heart on the inside of her right wrist and where every young man in the kingdom was born with a small arrow birthmark on the inside of his left wrist. In this land, young people took part in youth group activities, which were supported by their family and their church, while they matured physically, psychologically, spiritually and emotionally. When a boy and a girl were sufficiently matured and the girl spoke with the boy destined to be her spouse forever, the birthmarks would pulse and change color from blue to red. With this highly organized system, there was no doubt of one's destiny with the other, and, of course, there was no chance that marriage meant for a lifetime would end in divorce. Though that might sound appealing, think about what it would really mean. In that land there would be no risk of choice, no thrill of discovery.

Does that fable describe an ideal world? I think not. And God did not think so either, so we were created with free will and the responsibility of making life choices. The choice of a spouse is to be made carefully and for life. Both parties must realize the importance and the consequences of the choices made.

Unlike our throwaway society that sometimes views relationships as disposable, the Catholic Church has always highly valued marriage as the stable basis of the family unit. For the Catholic Church, marriage is not only the lifetime commitment of a man and a woman but also a holy union of which God is a part. Church teaching about marriage is very counter to our current media culture. Proper preparation for marriage is not a reality television stunt where a bachelor (or bachelorette) dates a series of willing women (or men) and dramatically selects one to wed. Marriage is not a promise to stay with this person as long as the relationship feels good.

The Catholic Church respects all marriage. When two people enter into marriage, Catholic or not, baptized or not, in a civil ceremony or a Church ritual, the spouses pledge fidelity to each other for life. Each wedding is a profound moment of lifetime commitment that should not be taken lightly. There is much to consider before scheduling the wedding, and more importantly, before beginning the lifetime commitment of Holy Matrimony. This section of the book offers some of the questions posed to the Marriage Room of OnceCatholic.org which focus on issues related to marriage preparation and weddings.

THE IMPORTANCE OF MARRIAGE

QUESTION: WHY IS IT SEEMINGLY SO DIFFICULT TO GET married in the Catholic Church? I am not married (I'm a member of a religious order) but have been disturbed for a long time regarding the marriage laws of our Church. How is it that they ever got so cumbersome?

What perseverance and determination individuals must possess to go through all of the details of marriage cases! It disturbs me to hear about someone hungry to come back to the Catholic Church, and even though we are welcoming, we lay down the "rules" of all the somewhat legal things they must do. We don't require this for any other types of things that might have drawn someone away from the Church. Why is this? We need to keep doing what we can to bring people to the place best suited for them to find their God. Sincerely, *Sister Ann*

RESPONSE: PROTECTING THE SANCTITY OF MARRIAGE IS WHAT IS truly important. I hear and share the compassion in your heart. But in that compassion, we must remember that joining or returning to the Church also means accepting the basic laws of the Church. A long-standing tradition in our Catholic Church is a profound respect for the sacrament of marriage. Like religious vows, the marital commitment should not be entered into lightly nor gotten out of lightly. The rules you find cumbersome are the Church's attempt to protect the sanctity of marriage, to respect the lifelong commitment marriage should be.

Yes, we as a Church want to welcome new and welcome back former members. However, that does not mean there are no consequences for choices that a person may have made in the past. Rules are just part of the price of being part of a very human group that brings us to divine grace—a group of people who are sinners who have a need to repent and make restitution before moving on freely with life. You know that as I do. Sometimes we just need a reminder that there are obligations that flow from membership as well as rights. *Sister Faith*

Preparation for Marriage

Q. My daughter has finally found the love of her life. Why does she need a priest to tell her anything about marriage? My daughter was raised Catholic, but did not want to marry. She had many problems with her "partner's" lack of fidelity. Many times she trusted him when he said it would never happen again. She finally broke up with that man and now she has met a wonderful young man and plans to marry this summer. They want their marriage in the Catholic Church. The priest is insisting that they go through many months of preparation for marriage, which is ridiculous since she already had the experience of living as if married with an unfaithful bum but now has found the love of her life and is quite sure of her decision to marry. I don't want to be disrespectful but I am angry, as is my daughter who is considering not bothering with the Church. *Alexis*

R. Marriage preparation is crucial and necessary for all those getting married. Your daughter's having lived with an unfaithful man for some time is the opposite of good preparation for choosing a spouse. She is likely to be on the rebound from that relationship, which could make the current "love of her life" seem much better than he is in reality. She needs even more preparation for marriage than if she had never cohabited before the wedding. She owes it to herself and the man she thinks she loves to do all she can to be sure they will have a lifelong marriage filled with commitment.

The Church needs to be sure there is no reason why this couple cannot marry each other so there will be a careful investigation that neither has been married before or there is no other canonical (Church law) impediment to prevent the wedding. Both intended spouses need to be properly instructed about what the Church means by marriage which is very different from the idea of marriage rampant in our culture, especially in television shows and movies as well as many novels. Good communication is essential for a good marriage, and the preparation will include opportunities for those skilled in such matters to observe this couple and advise them about respecting each other as well as determining whether they share similar values about commitment, children, permanence, etc. Marriage is a commitment for life not to be entered into without serious discernment and preparation. I hope you will encourage your daughter to cooperate and not be in a rush to wed. Have her meet with the priest at the parish where she intends to marry to begin the preparation. It is important that she resolve any issues from the past (particularly the cohabitation and experience of betrayal that infidelity was for her) before entering a new one so the new one has the best chance. I will be praying for both of you. *Sister Faith*

Q. DO MY SECOND HUSBAND-TO-BE AND I HAVE TO ATTEND pre-Cana counseling before we can be married in the Church? *Sandra*

R. PREPARATION FOR MARRIAGE (PRE-CANA) IS EVEN MORE necessary when marrying for the second time. If your first marriage is declared null (see further discussion of this process in Chapter 3), you and your intended spouse will be required to complete the requirements of your diocese for marriage preparation. Some people think that because they have been married before such preparation is not necessary. Actually, the opposite is true—preparation is even more necessary. In the U.S. about fifty percent of first marriages fail while an even higher percentage of second marriage attempts fail. It is very important that you be sure neither of you is bringing "baggage" from your failed marriage into the new one and that you are truly choosing each other for a lifetime commitment. Be patient with yourselves and the process.

In nearly all cases the priest or deacon will want to meet with you and your intended spouse for premarital discussions. The number of meetings and issues will depend on your situation. I try to tailor the premarital preparation for each unique situation. May God bless you. *Father Mike*

Q. CAN MY FIANCÉ AND I TAKE PRE-CANA AT SEPARATE parishes? I will be getting married within the next six months and I know that we have to take classes with the Church before the actual ceremony. My questions are the following: Is it mandatory that we attend those classes together? I live three hundred and fifty miles from my fiancée, and it is not possible that we take the classes together. Can I take my preparation class here at my parish while she takes her class at her parish? Thank you for your time and God bless. *Manny*

R. I SUGGEST YOU CALL THE PRIEST OR DEACON WHO WILL BE presiding at your wedding ceremony. This would be his decision. Based on my experience, there may be some things that you could do separately, but I would suspect that there would be some things the priest or deacon would want you to do together. Some of that would be "negotiable" (that's my word) based on the length of time you've been dating, how old you are, whether or not you lived for a time in the same city or town as your intended spouse, whether you are of the same faith tradition, whether either of you were married before, whether either of you has children, etc. I hope this helps. Please write if you have further questions. May God bless you both. I'll keep you in my prayers. *Father Mike*

Cohabitation before Marriage

Q. IF A MAN LIVES WITH HIS GIRLFRIEND IN THE SAME HOUSE and they intend to get married, can they receive Holy Communion during Mass or are they not allowed to until they get married officially in the Church? *Dominic*

R. LIVING TOGETHER IN THE SAME HOUSE DOES NOT LIMIT ONE in receiving Holy Communion. Having sexual intercourse before/outside of marriage, which is sometimes presumed for people who are living together, is what limits one in receiving Holy Communion. Sexual intercourse before/outside of marriage is a mortal sin. Statistics (these are not accumulated by people hired by the Church, but by sociologists doing research) show that people living together before marriage, with or without sexual intercourse, have a much higher rate of divorce. Thanks for writing. Please know that I make no judgments of your relationship as I offer this response. You and your loved ones will be in my prayers. *Father Mike*

RULES FOR HOLY COMMUNION AT A CATHOLIC WEDDING

Q. WHAT IS THE RULE FOR NON-CATHOLICS IN ATTENDANCE at a Catholic wedding? May they participate in Holy Communion? We are getting married in May. We are both Catholic, and I have a question about Holy Communion at our wedding. I was always under the impression that a non-Catholic should not receive Holy Communion at a Catholic Mass. My fiancé says he has been to a couple of weddings at which Holy Communion was offered to all who wanted to participate. Is this true? *Marilyn*

R. THE BISHOPS OF THE UNITED STATES HAVE SET SOME clear guidelines on the reception of the Eucharist by non-Catholics. Usually you will find these regulations on the inside cover of the missalettes that are in most Catholic Church pews. Because Catholics believe that the celebration of Eucharist is a sign of the reality of the oneness of faith and worship, members of churches that are not fully united with the Roman Catholic Church are ordinarily not allowed to receive Holy Communion. For very rare and special circumstances there may be permission that has to be obtained from the diocesan bishop for a Christian person to receive Communion on a particular occasion. Non-Christians may never receive Communion. *Father Francis*

VALID AND SACRAMENTAL MARRIAGE

Q. I HAVE OFTEN SEEN MARRIAGES REFERRED TO AS EITHER valid or sacramental. Is there a difference between a valid marriage and a sacramental marriage? Can you have a valid marriage that is not sacramental? *Cindy*

R. NOT ALL VALID MARRIAGES ARE SACRAMENTAL ONES. For the sacrament of marriage, the ministers are the couple themselves (the priest or deacon is an official witness necessary for Catholics) so if the members of a couple are not baptized (remember baptism is the gateway to the sacraments of the Church) then their marriage is a valid one, but not a sacramental one. *Sister Faith*

Q. WHAT KIND OF MARRIAGE (VALID OR SACRAMENTAL) would it have been if neither party was baptized? You stated that there would be a decision whether or not there was clear evidence that something essential was missing in the marriage from the moment of consent that prevented it from becoming a sacrament (for the baptized). *Carl*

R. IF TWO NEVER-BAPTIZED PEOPLE MARRY, THAT MARRIAGE cannot be sacramental because baptism is required before all other sacraments. This would be presumed to be a valid natural marriage binding for life. *Sister Faith*

Q. HOW CAN THERE BE A SACRAMENTAL MARRIAGE WITH no church and no priest? My son received one dispensation in order to have the ceremony in a private location. I believe my son is waiting for a reply for another dispensation for someone other than a priest to officiate. The priest told him he was not allowed to officiate since it was not in a church. I am confused. *Mary*

R. IN THE TEACHING OF THE ROMAN CATHOLIC CHURCH, the union of a couple in a marriage is a sacrament because of the consent of the couple, that is, the bride and the groom. In other words, the bride and the groom are the ministers of the sacrament to each other. This is because they are the ones who promise to be true to each other in good times and in bad, in sickness and in health, until death. Neither the presence of a priest presiding at the ceremony, nor the location of the ceremony, makes the marriage a sacrament. The priest is the official witness of the Catholic Church that the marriage has occurred. If the "form of marriage" is dispensed, then someone else is named as the official witness. *Father Mike*

Q. IF THE "MINISTERS" OF THE SACRAMENT OF MATRIMONY are the bride and groom, is a marriage valid without a priest or a deacon? In the thread on valid and sacramental issues, I have read that the ministers of the sacrament of matrimony are the bride and groom. But, it also seems to indicate that the marriage is not valid unless there is a priest or deacon acting as an official witness.

This issue concerns me because I am a Catholic who is planning on marrying a Baptist in the Baptist Church in about a year. It would be nice for the marriage to be recognized by all Christians, and it seems it should be because we (my fiancée and myself) will be the ministers and will give ourselves freely to one another. Many Catholics, Baptists, and those of other denominations will be in attendance and they will surely look at this as a valid marriage. If I invite a priest or a deacon to come and witness the ceremony (in the pews with everyone else), will the marriage be recognized in the eyes of the Roman Catholic Church? It just seems to me there are so many rules and caveats that don't seem necessary. God bless, *Brian*

R. CATHOLICS ONLY ARE OBLIGED TO THE RULES OF THE Church about proper form for marriage. In order for a marriage to be valid, a priest or a deacon must preside at the wedding ceremony. In some cases, Church permission is given for a Catholic to marry before a non-Catholic minister (for example a father of the bride is a Protestant minister, and the couple has gone through Catholic marriage preparation and wishes to marry in her father's church with him presiding). In this case, a couple may receive a "dispensation" by the Church to be married by a non-Catholic minister. A priest sitting in a pew attending a wedding does not meet the requirements for canonical form.

Only Catholics are obliged to canonical form. Every marriage is presumed by Catholic Church law to be a valid union unless the contrary is proven. One way for a marriage to be invalid for a Catholic is if that Catholic did not marry according to Church rules for marriage.

You mention that you would like all Christian churches to recognize your planned marriage. For it to be valid for you as a Catholic, you need to meet with a priest at your parish to arrange for marriage preparation and then to see if there are reasons why you might be permitted to marry your intended spouse in her Baptist church. I hope you will do that. God's blessings, *Sister Faith*

Q. IF A MAN AND A WOMAN DO NOT HAVE SEXUAL RELATIONS, is their marriage still valid? I have been married for eight years and we have three small children. My husband has multiple sclerosis. We have not had sexual relations in over two years. He is ten years older than me. We are converts to the Catholic Church, and we married in the Catholic Church. I am constantly tempted by other men. I want to feel passion and love that I don't have with my husband, try as I may. I feel like I am living with my brother. I go to confession often but I am afraid I will just break down and do something shameful. If sexual relations are not a part of a marriage, is it still a valid marriage? *Carla*

R. A QUICK ANSWER TO YOUR QUESTION IS YES; YOUR marriage is a valid one. But there is a larger issue here: your unhappiness. I believe that you need to sit down and talk with a counselor or at least your parish priest. I will keep you and your husband in my prayers. *Father Francis*

MIXED RELIGIONS AND MARRIAGE

Q. I AM NOT A CATHOLIC, BUT I AM DATING A MAN WHO IS Catholic. I am unfamiliar with the Catholic faith, and I would like to learn more about what it will take to marry a Catholic. What things should I know about and understand beforehand? I love him regardless and the differences of religion do not matter to us, but what about the Church? How will the Church or even his family view him or us when they find out I am not Catholic? Is this a big deal? *Lacey*

R. WHEN A CATHOLIC MARRIES A NON-CATHOLIC, SOME OF THE basic rules for a Catholic marriage are:

1) All Catholics must marry in ceremonies recognized by the Catholic Church. If they don't marry in the Catholic Church with a deacon, priest or bishop presiding, they must get special permission (the official term is a *dispensation*) to marry elsewhere. For example, this past month I assisted a Catholic to receive a dispensation to marry in a Presbyterian church.

2) Both the man and the woman must be free to marry. For example, neither has been married before this wedding.

3) The Catholic person is asked to sign a statement reaffirming his or her faith in Jesus Christ with the intention of continuing to live that faith in the Catholic Church; the Catholic party also promises to do all in his or her power to share the faith by having children baptized and raised in the Catholic faith.

4) There will probably be some type of marriage preparation process with the parish priest or others.

5) The marriage must be open to children, and the parties have to intend to be faithful and married until death.

It is possible for a Catholic to marry a non-Catholic. But there may be differences in faith traditions that need to be discussed and resolved before the wedding. The parish priest may assist in that discussion. Please know that the next two wedding ceremonies that I will be part of involve a Catholic and a non-Catholic.

Unfortunately, I can't speak for how his family will react. But, I will pray for both of you. Peace, *Father Mike*

Q. MY WIFE AND I ARE ALREADY MARRIED, BUT WE WANT our marriage to be recognized by the Church. Where do we begin? I was not practicing my faith so I married outside of the Church. My wife is not Catholic but she is willing to do a Church wedding for me. *Anthony*

R. FOR YOUR MARRIAGE TO BE RECOGNIZED, YOU NEED TO have a new wedding that will be according to Church law this time. This can be a quiet ceremony with you and your spouse before a priest or a deacon and two witnesses. This is called a convalidation. It is important that you both realize this is a new act of consent and that your valid marriage begins now for you as a Catholic. Welcome back, *Sister Faith*

Q. WHAT IS A DISPENSATION? WHY DO I (A CATHOLIC) NEED a dispensation to marry a once Catholic, but now newly baptized Baptist? My priest tells me I need a dispensation for mixed religions to marry my fiancé. I am a bit uneasy about all of this getting permission to even marry the man whom I feel God sent for me to marry. My fiancé also feels this way and it seems that there is more support in his congregation for our marriage. Please help me understand why, if my fiancé and I are truly in love and want to start a family in God's name, is it necessary to get permission from the Church? *Ruby*

R. YOU MAY NOT BE AWARE OF THIS, BUT EVERY TIME A Catholic marries a baptized non-Catholic, the Church must grant permission. The concern is that the Catholic party will be unable to continue in the practice of his/her faith. Since there are many wedding ceremonies between Catholics and baptized non-Catholics, the permission is granted with great frequency.

And sometimes, when people leave the Catholic Church, they are bitter and/or hostile toward the Catholic Church. I have talked with some people who are hateful toward the Catholic Church. I am not judging their motives and reasons, and this may not pertain to your fiancé. But the permission that is granted is done so after some discussion and with some assurance that you will be able to continue in your Catholic faith. From what you have noted, it seems this would be important to you.

The recommendation of a priest accompanies the request for permission. Blessings to you and your fiancé! *Father Mike*

Q. WE RECENTLY ATTENDED A WORLD WIDE MARRIAGE Encounter given by my diocese. The priest that celebrated Mass included a renewal of vows and a blessing of marriages. My husband thinks this counts as a blessing of our marriage, but I am not certain. Can you please clarify? My husband and I were married in a nondenominational church. It was a first marriage for both of us. I am a cradle Catholic baptized and confirmed. My husband is not baptized and does not practice a formal religion. My pastor says that we still need to have our marriage blessed. *Tina*

R. AS FAR AS THE CATHOLIC CHURCH IS CONCERNED, YOU ARE not married validly. As a Catholic you are obliged to canonical form, which you did not observe at your wedding. You need more than a blessing for your current civil union. You need a whole new act of consent according to Church law, called a convalidation. Please talk soon with a priest about getting married in the Church. God's blessings, *Sister Faith*

GETTING MARRIED OUTSIDE THE CHURCH

Q. HOW WOULD GOD LOOK AT ME FOR GETTING MARRIED outside the Church? We intend to marry in the Church as soon as his marriage case is completed. If I die in the meantime, do I go to hell? As I have read on this site, the civil marriage is still a valid marriage. Does this mean we are not committing adultery? I want to receive Holy Communion, but I also love this man dearly. *Katherine*

R. THE CATHOLIC CHURCH TEACHING ON DIVORCE AND remarriage comes from the Bible and is based on the teaching of the Son of God. In Matthew 19:3-9, Jesus taught that what God has joined in marriage, man must not divide. In Matthew 5:31-32, Jesus taught that a man who divorces his wife forces her to commit adultery, and the man who marries a divorced woman likewise commits adultery. The Church understands that these teachings pertaining to divorce and remarriage apply to both men and women.

A Catholic who marries outside the Church may not receive Holy Communion. According to Catholic Church teaching, the scenario you describe would be an adulterous relationship. This is due to the Church's teaching on marriage and divorce, which is summarized above. According to the Bible and Church teaching, adultery is a grave sin. Those who have committed grave sins, whether it is adultery or another grave sin, are not permitted to receive Holy Communion.

In the law of the Church, all marriages are valid until proven otherwise. But that only matters if one is trying to prove that a marriage is invalid in a tribunal process, which is further described in Chapter 3 of this book. The bottom line is that if you married outside the Church and you are seeking a declaration of nullity from a tribunal, the presumption is that your marriage is valid unless it is proven otherwise.

There is an old story that I heard some time ago. A wise and elderly priest was talking with someone. Every time the person asked a question about heaven and God, the priest responded, "I don't know." After this happened several times, the exasperated person exclaimed, "Don't you know anything about God?" The priest said, "Oh, yes. There are two things about God that I know. First, there is a God. And second, I'm not God." I can't tell you how God would look at you if you marry outside the Church. And God will be your final judge, not me. I hope and pray that God is merciful with each of us. I am not judging you as I type this answer. God is our Judge. I will keep you and your intended spouse in my prayers. *Father Mike*

Q. I WAS MARRIED TWO YEARS AGO IN A CIVIL CEREMONY TO A non-Catholic. I want to be able to go to Mass and receive Holy Communion but I am not sure of my rights. Please, can anyone help me? I have attended Mass and received Eucharist and now I find out I should not have done that. My husband will not convert to being Catholic. *Avril*

R. A CONVALIDATION OR A RADICAL SANATION WOULD PERMIT you to again receive the Sacraments. I am presuming that the civil ceremony is the only wedding ceremony for you or your husband. That is, neither of you had been married before your marriage to each other took place. If either of you was married before, my answer would be different.

In order to practice your faith fully as a Catholic, there are two ways for your marriage to be recognized by the

Church. The first is known as a simple convalidation, which requires your consent to marriage at this time. In my experience, a simple convalidation ceremony is a brief ceremony with a few family members or friends present as witnesses and a priest or deacon. Or, the second way for you to regularize your marriage is a radical sanation. A radical sanation does not require a new act of consent (if, for example, your husband intends to continue your marriage but believes you are already validly married and refuses to go through a quiet Church ceremony with you). This would be granted by a Church official. Your parish priest should be able to assist you with either the simple convalidation or the radical sanation.

Your husband does not have to become a Catholic in order for your marriage to be recognized by the Catholic Church. Peace, *Father Mike*

GETTING MARRIED "OUTSIDE" OF A CHURCH

Q. DO I HAVE TO GET MARRIED INSIDE AN ACTUAL CHURCH? I am Catholic and engaged to a man who was baptized Catholic but does not practice his faith and rejects organized religion. I had been a practicing Catholic up until a few years ago. It is important to me to be married in the Catholic faith, and my fiancé has no problem participating in a Catholic ceremony. However, we both deeply want an outdoor ceremony: me, because I have always felt closest to God in nature; and him, because he is not comfortable in churches (although he is willing to have the ceremony in a church if that is what I want). As I look into the possibility of an outdoor ceremony, I am becoming more and more angry with the Church and its rigidity. Whatever happened to Jesus' "For where two or three are gathered in my name, there I am in the midst of them" (Matthew 8:20)? Why won't the presence of a priest and a congregation of our loved ones create a church? I believe it does. I am so torn with wanting to totally reject the Catholic Church but not wanting a wedding ceremony that is faithless. To me God joins two people in marriage, and I don't consider a civil ceremony an option. I'd appreciate any insight that you could give me. Thank you very much, *Sara*

R. ONE OF THE LAWS OF THE CHURCH, CANON 1118, STATES that the marriage of Catholics is to take place in a parish church. But the local ordinary (diocesan bishop) may permit marriage to be celebrated in another suitable place. It is my understanding that most Catholic bishops will not permit outdoor wedding ceremonies. I'm told that their concern stems from whether or not the place is suitable for a sacred, religious celebration. A parish church is a sacred space. Some would call these bishops rigid. I would like to add that you are right that God joins two people together in marriage. Or said another way, it takes three to marry: a man, a woman and Christ. And you are right that Jesus said that where two or three are gathered in His name, He is in their midst.

But I'll give you a couple of examples of why the Church might doubt one's choice of possible sanctified marriage places outside of the church, from my own personal experience. First, I am told that certain civil judges in the city in which I live will not perform wedding ceremonies outside their chambers. I don't know why, but I suppose they may be concerned about the suitability of the place the couple has in mind. Second, several months ago, I was visiting a friend in a large city. On my way to meet him for lunch, someone stopped me. From my clothing, it was clear I was a priest. He asked me if I was coming to the courthouse for the wedding. I asked, "What wedding?" He said a radio station had given a wedding as a prize, and the couple was getting married in a portable restroom. The ceremony was open to the public, and he was going. I think you get the picture. What seems suitable for one person may be distasteful for another.

Once again, a parish church is certainly an appropriate space for a holy, sacramental wedding ceremony. I would suspect the place you have in mind is beautiful. After all, God created it. I would suggest you contact your parish priest and ask him about the possibility of having your wedding where you would like. The odds are (I want to be honest with you) you won't be able to have a Catholic ceremony there. But perhaps you can use the space for wedding pictures, for your reception, or in celebrating your first wedding anniversary and other special occasions.

I will keep you in my prayers. May God bless you and your fiancé and deepen your love for each other. Peace,
Father Mike

BECOMING A CATHOLIC BEFORE MARRIAGE

Q. I AM A PRACTICING CATHOLIC BUT MY FIANCÉ IS NOT; he has never been baptized into any religion. How do we go about getting married in the Church and arrange for his entry into the Church? I would like to marry in the Catholic Church, and he is very keen to enter the Catholic faith, having gone to church several times with me. *Abigail*

R. CONGRATULATIONS ON YOUR DECISION TO ENTER MARRIAGE in the Catholic Church and I am pleased to learn that your fiancé also wishes to enter the Church.

You should enroll in a parish where you live. When you register, inform the parish representative that you would like to set up a meeting with the pastor about a date for marriage. You should also inquire about the Rite of Christian Initiation for Adults (RCIA) program in the parish. Congratulations and good luck! *Father Francis*

BECOMING A CATHOLIC AFTER MARRIAGE

Q. I WAS MARRIED TWO YEARS AGO IN A PROTESTANT ceremony. I am Protestant, and my husband is a cradle Catholic who drifted away from the Church some years ago after the death of his mother. What do I need to do to make our marriage valid in the Catholic faith?

I have prayed long and hard as to how we can find a way to raise our children to know God in a community of faith, and it has come to me that the way is for me to explore becoming Catholic. It was only once I mentioned that I would be willing to explore this that my husband seemed to become interested in going to church again. As a Protestant I was raised to believe that all Christian churches are really one in their faith in Christ. I feel that God has been leading me to this. I do not want to be the sole churchgoer when we have children. It is hard to teach them to love God if one parent does not live in faith.

However, I am nervous about this very issue that you mention. Assuming all goes well and I go through Rite of Christian Initiation for Adults (RCIA), I assume it is not until after that point that we could go through the process of having our marriage recognized in the Catholic Church.

I am concerned that I will become pregnant before I am able to go through all of the necessary procedures and that our child will be considered "born out of wedlock" and that the child's baptism will have to be delayed. *Selina*

R. THERE IS NO NEED FOR YOU TO BECOME CATHOLIC BEFORE you can marry validly in the Catholic Church. You will just need to complete required preparation for a Catholic marriage with your current spouse. You begin by meeting with a priest at the parish you will attend.

Before or after the convalidation, you can begin your own process of instruction in the faith. Since you mention that your husband has fallen away from the Church after the death of his mother, let me suggest you ask him to accompany you to your instruction sessions so he may rekindle his faith, and you can both share about what you are learning. If you have a child before you have completed the process of becoming Catholic, you will be able to have that child baptized Catholic. May God bless you in your efforts to create a faith-filled home and bless you with happy and healthy children. *Sister Faith*

Q. I AM THINKING ABOUT A RETURN TO THE CATHOLIC CHURCH after a long absence. I have been married for eleven years to a non-Catholic and have two children. Will I also need to be remarried in the Catholic Church? A Justice of the Peace married us. I am planning to have my children baptized soon. Can this be a simple process? Will my husband have to convert? *Annice*

R. WELCOME BACK! IF YOU HAVE NOT LEFT THE CHURCH BY a formal and public act such as being baptized in another religion, you do need to marry in the Church. This will be a convalidation, which is a new act of marital consent, provided your spouse is willing to go through this Catholic wedding with you. If he wants to remain married to you but is unwilling to go through a new act of consent in a Catholic wedding, you could talk with the priest at your parish about applying for a radical sanation (healing at the root) where Church authority heals your consent after promises from you and after evidence that your spouse intends to remain married to you. He does not need to convert but I hope he will support your practicing your faith and having your children baptized Catholic. Meet with a priest soon to arrange for the baptisms of your children and to straighten out your marriage situation. Again, welcome back.
Sister Faith

Q. I WAS MARRIED OUT OF THE CATHOLIC CHURCH. I LOVE my husband dearly, and he loves me, but he will not go through a Church wedding. Help! *Jo*

R. IF THERE ARE NO BARRIERS TO MARRIAGE WITH YOUR current civil spouse such as either of you being married before, there is a way your marriage can become valid without a Church wedding.

This is called a radical sanation. You would need to complete some papers with a priest at your parish explaining the facts of your situation and asking the bishop to radically sanate (heal at the root) your marriage. Such a sanation would depend on your explaining why you are sure your current civil spouse intends to continue your marriage but just resists a Church ceremony. Ask your parish priest about this. Blessings on your return to the Church.
Sister Faith

REJOINING THE CHURCH

Q. I WOULD LIKE TO COME HOME TO THE CHURCH AS WELL. Given my experience in life and the need to experience God's love and forgiveness, this is very important to me. Is there a place for me here? My entire family is Catholic except for my aunt and her family. I received my religious education in her Protestant church. While I was in college I joined the Catholic Church. This process included weekly instructions at the parish and I received the sacraments.

During that time I met my husband who is not Catholic, and we married without the blessing of the Catholic Church.

No story is ever simple and neither is mine. After three children and eighteen years of marriage, we divorced. I then married another man and we joined the Presbyterian Church in our city. We were married for almost four years when we divorced. I then asked my first husband and the father of my children to allow me to come home where I belonged, and we have remarried.

I have been to many different churches over the years and have never felt the spiritual satisfaction and closeness to God I felt while attending the Catholic Church. I would like to come home to the Church as well. Is there a place for me here? *Helen*

R. YES, THERE IS DEFINITELY A PLACE FOR YOU IN THE Catholic Church. You need to speak with a priest in your area who understands the laws of the Catholic Church on marriage as well as some of the real life issues that surround divorce and reconciliation.

You did not mention if your first husband was previously married. If he was not, the process might be relatively simple from a Church point of view. From a relationship point of view, both you and he have hurt each other and some talking with a skilled professional might be beneficial.

But, as I said, most definitely there is a place for you in the Catholic Church. I will keep you in my prayers that you are able to follow up on your hopes. *Father Francis*

EXTENUATING CIRCUMSTANCES

Q. MY QUESTION IS CAN MY FIANCÉ AND I STILL GET MARRIED in the Catholic Church even though we have a baby together? *Jolene*

R. ALREADY HAVING A CHILD OUT OF WEDLOCK DOES NOT mean you could not marry in the Church. Meet with a priest at the parish you attend to arrange for premarital preparation. Actually it is better not to rush into marriage before the child is born but to take the time to prepare for marriage and be sure that is what you want without the pressure of pregnancy at the time of your discerning. What is best for the child will be to grow up in the midst of a healthy marriage freely chosen by the spouses, not a hurried rush to wed before the child's birth. God's blessings on your life journey and on your child. *Sister Faith*

Q. IF A CATHOLIC MAN AND A CATHOLIC WOMAN ARE engaged to be married in the Catholic Church next year, and she gets pregnant and has the baby before the wedding, would they still be able to get married in the Church? What would need to happen for that to occur? (Obviously, the Church looks on premarital sex as a sin although many people do it and still marry in the Church.) *Mae*

R. THERE IS NO CHURCH LAW IMPEDIMENT THAT LIMITS OR changes your being married in the Church after having a child. If I were the priest involved in the marriage preparation, I would have some discussions with you that I would not have ordinarily because you are now parents. In particular, I would talk with you about having a child and the effect on your relationship as a new husband and wife. Also, the diocese in which you live may have special counseling for couples who are parents before marriage. A priest has to assess the readiness of both people to marry. With some couples, I could foresee the priest suggesting the wedding ceremony be postponed.

With all couples I meet, I encourage them to receive the sacrament of reconciliation during their courtship and before their wedding. If the pregnancy led a couple to become engaged and begin planning a wedding (which does not seem to be your situation), as the priest I would have concerns about the couple being able to freely choose marriage. I would be concerned that one or both of the parents feel they are being forced into marriage because it is the right thing to do rather than marrying because it is right to marry. You'll be in my prayers. *Father Mike*

PART 2:
DIVORCE AND THE CATHOLIC CHURCH

For several years in the 1990s, Bishop Carl K. Moeddel and I went around the Archdiocese of Cincinnati offering seminars that we called "We Miss You" evenings for those separated from the Church over marriage-related issues. He would include in his part of the presentation the statistics that one hundred years ago only four percent of marriages failed. Ninety-six percent of marriages lasted until the death of one of the spouses. Then the Bishop would indicate the pastoral problem that led to us offering such evenings. More recent statistics showed that approximately fifty percent of marriages fail. However one generates or uses statistics, it is clear that there are many more divorces today than there were one hundred years ago. With years of experience as a pastor, Bishop Moeddel knows well the pastoral problems that divorce raises for Catholics.

For Catholics, divorce does not end a marriage, and divorce does not remove a person from full membership in the Catholic Church. A divorced Catholic may still receive Holy Communion provided he or she has not attempted to marry again outside Church law. In 2003 Pope John Paul II did not change the Church's law when he simply restated that to receive Holy Communion one must be in full communion with the Church. A Catholic who attempts marriage outside the Church is not in full communion and so is not free to receive Eucharist. I think you will see that the Companions to the Marriage Room try to be as pastoral as possible while also "telling it like it is." As many parents know, true love is tough love that does not always make one feel good. It involves calling each of us to live up to the obligations we have made in our life choices.

Years ago, divorced Catholics felt excluded by their Church. Perhaps this is best illustrated in one older woman who came up after Bishop Moeddel and I had finished our presentations for one of the "We Miss You" evenings. She began by saying, "When I left the Church more than thirty years ago, no bishop would have spent an evening with a group of divorced people." Then she turned to me and continued, "Then he introduced you as the real expert about Church law. And you are a woman. That would never have happened thirty years ago." In some confusion, she added, "Then you proceeded to tease him with examples during your talk and he clearly responded positively." With tears flowing, she concluded, "This is a Church I want to come back to." I hope those of you reading this book will also feel invited back by the responses of the Companions to this site. Returning to full practice of your faith will not always be an easy path, but I pray it will be a worthwhile one for you.

CATHOLIC "STATUS" AFTER A DIVORCE

Q. WHY DOES THE CATHOLIC CHURCH MAKE IT SO DIFFICULT for divorced Catholics to remain Catholics? I have four children, all divorced and out of the Catholic Church. My children refuse to present marriage cases. They feel that their Catholic marriages did happen, and a declaration of nullity is nothing more than a lie. The whole process is ridiculous. *Emma*

R. THE FACT THAT YOUR CHILDREN HAVE BEEN DIVORCED DOES not put them out of the Church or cause any problem with them remaining full practicing Catholics. Only if they choose to ignore the lifetime commitments they made in marriage and marry again outside the Church without having the first marriage declared null, will they be unable to receive the sacraments. However, they are still able to attend Mass weekly and practice their faith as far as they are able. When one we love is suffering, it is easy to say, "Change the rules!" but that does not generate good decisions. The Church is trying to protect the value of marriage, not to demean the commitment you yourself are living out. *Sister Faith*

HOLY COMMUNION AFTER DIVORCE

Q. WHY CAN'T I RECEIVE HOLY COMMUNION? I AM A divorced Catholic. My ex-husband left our young child and me. I have since remarried outside the Church. My husband

and I feel God brought us together. We attend the Catholic Church regularly, and my daughter is getting ready to make her first confession in a few weeks. We are raising our children in the Church, and we feel we are very good Christian people. So why am I to be punished for the failure of my first marriage? I am having a very hard time understanding this. Some people say if I feel so strongly about it then I should receive Holy Communion anyway. Isn't this a Catholic rule? Is it written anywhere in the Bible or did Jesus actually say we cannot receive Holy Communion because of a divorce? I think Jesus took me and my child out of an unhappy home and gave us what we have now, which is a very loving family. Please help me to understand this particular rule because this is something so very important to me. Sincerely, *Sandra*

R. IT IS EVIDENT THAT THE LORD IS IN YOUR LIFE, BUT FROM what you told me, you may not participate in Holy Communion. Please know that I am not judging you as I respond to you. It is not written in the Bible that someone who is divorced may not receive Holy Communion. In fact, a divorced person may receive Holy Communion. A divorced and remarried Catholic or a Catholic who is married to someone who has been married previously may not receive Holy Communion unless they have received a declaration of nullity for the first marriage, and their new marriage is recognized by the Church.

This is due to the Church's teaching on marriage and divorce. According to Church teaching, a person who divorces and remarries without the benefit of a declaration of nullity is in a state of public adultery. This is based on the teaching of Jesus in Matthew's Gospel that someone who divorces and remarries another commits adultery (Matthew 19:9). According to the Bible and Church teaching, adultery is a grave sin. Those who are in grave sin are not permitted to receive Holy Communion.

I am happy that you and your child are in a loving home. I would encourage you to seek a declaration of nullity and to have your marriage recognized by the Church. A declaration of nullity seeks to determine if your first marriage was valid in the eyes of the Church. It is not a judgment of you as a person. I hope this helps. You and your loved ones will be in my prayers. *Father Mike*

DIVORCE DOES NOT MEAN EXCOMMUNICATION

Q. IF I MARRY A DIVORCED MAN, WILL I BE EXCOMMUNICATED? Will Holy Communion be withheld from me? I have known this man for almost five years now. When we first met he had only been divorced for several months. He is agnostic, and has no desire to become active in any faith again. His divorce was due to adultery on his wife's part. From what he has told me, he made a good effort to keep the marriage together. *Victoria*

R. IF YOU MARRY HIM, YOU WOULD NOT BE EXCOMMUNICATED. If you marry him, the teaching of the Church is that you should not receive Holy Communion. This is due to the Church's teaching on marriage and divorce. According to

Church teaching, a person who marries someone who is divorced and who has not received a declaration of nullity is in a state of permanent and public adultery. This is based on the teaching of Jesus in Matthew's Gospel that someone who divorces and marries another commits adultery, as mentioned previously (Matthew 19:9). According to the Bible and Church teaching, adultery is a grave sin. Those who have committed grave sins, whether that is adultery or other grave sins, are not permitted to receive Holy Communion. I'll keep you in my prayers. *Father Mike*

CONSEQUENCES OF CHOICE

Q. WHY SHOULD I BE PUNISHED BECAUSE MY HUSBAND'S FIRST wife ended their marriage? My husband has been divorced from his first marriage for twenty-seven years. We have been married for twenty-five years. I want so much to be a part of the Catholic Church again. *Garnet*

R. WHAT YOU REFER TO AS BEING PUNISHED I WOULD CALL suffering the consequences of your choices. You are the one who chose to marry a divorced man out of the Church, which is the reason you may not fully participate in the sacramental life of the Church today.

I hope you will encourage your civil spouse to present a marriage case to find out if you will be able to marry in the Church and return to the sacraments. *Sister Faith*

Q. CAN I RETURN TO THE CHURCH AFTER A DIVORCE? MY wife and I were married in the Catholic Church when I was twenty and she was nineteen. We kept the stormy relationship going for many long years until I filed for divorce. We spoke with a priest at the time we were trying to reconcile and he said we were too immature when we married. I drifted away from the Church and have not been to Mass since I began the divorce. Even though I am the one who filed for divorce I felt I did not get much support from my priest to keep the marriage going when he said our marriage was not a sound one from the beginning.

I am very interested in resuming the practice of my faith but I feel out of place now and would not be comfortable seeing that same priest. I feel he took sides against my marriage. *Vernon*

R. You may approach any priest to assist you in returning to the sacraments. As long as you have not attempted to marry again outside the Church, you are free to return to the sacraments despite being divorced. Please contact another priest to help you come back to the Church. He can also help you present a case to see if your first marriage can be declared null. Welcome back. **Sister Faith**

When Your Spouse Leaves

Q. Is the Church telling us that if your spouse leaves you for someone else, then that is not a reason that one should be allowed to remarry in the Church? I am asking on behalf of a friend of mine whose spouse left her for another woman. It just seems that this happens to too many people

today. My friend and I both find it hard to believe that the
Catholic Church is not going to let all of these people who
were left high and dry by an ex-spouse marry again in the
Church. It does not make any sense to me. Over 50 percent
of first marriages end in divorce, which is a lot of people out
there!

I know, I know, the whole marriage case thing is to
prove that the marriage should not have taken place from
the beginning. But it did. Are you saying that for many who
married, tribunals can find reasons why they should not
have married in the first place? I know I am sure there are
some very obvious cases of invalid marriages but for the
most part, come on! I just don't get this. *Kim*

R. YOU HAVE HIT ON THE KEY IDEA: WHEN A PERSON MARRIES
(Catholic or not, in a church or not) it is a lifetime
commitment, a pledge to be married to that person for the
rest of your life. If a spouse chooses to leave, that does not
remove the commitment. Your very shock at the idea only
shows how much our society has come to condone divorce
and remarriage.

I think if more people realized this is a commitment for
life, they might be more careful to be sure of their
commitment, date longer to be sure they know the other
person well enough to make the commitment, and realize
that if that spouse were to leave them, they would not be
free to marry again if the first marriage is a valid one. It is a
tremendously serious commitment that is often not
respected as such.

If the Church declares a marriage invalid it means that there is proof that something essential was missing from the beginning moment, the time of consent, which prevented the marriage from being a valid one. Unfortunately, there are quite a number of invalid marriages in the United States these days.

If you are considering making a marital commitment yourself, I hope you will take the time necessary to be sure of your decision. I also hope you will continue to support your friend as she goes through the tribunal process. Waiting is a large part of her role. If she is intending to marry again, I hope she will use this time to be sure she is making a mature judgment about a commitment that will be for the rest of her life if her first marriage is declared null. God's blessings on both of you. *Sister Faith*

PART 3:
TRIBUNAL PROCESSES

The man was frustrated when the Judges for his case asked for more witnesses. He called me as Director of the Tribunal asking, "Sister, what do I need to do to have you just make my marriage disappear? Can't you just make it null and void?" I tried to explain to him that we do not make marriages null. The tribunal process might declare that a marriage was null from the very beginning, but the Judges do not make a valid marriage invalid. Every marriage is presumed to be valid according to Catholic Church law (canon 1060). For that presumption to be overturned, there needs to be sufficient proof, and anything the Petitioner says needs to be corroborated by documents or the testimony of witnesses.

Divorce does not end marriage according to Catholic teaching, but there are some ways that a person might be free to marry again according to Catholic Church law. In their responses in this section, the Companions will explain

Lack of Form cases, Pauline Privilege cases, Ligamen cases, Favor of the Faith cases, and Formal cases seeking a declaration of nullity. It is possible that something the Church considers essential to valid marriage was missing from a particular union at the time of consent that prevented it from becoming a union binding for life and, for the baptized, prevented it from becoming a sacrament.

The tribunal process is the area where most of the questions to the Web site are focused. We have chosen a sampling of these questions to help you understand the process. It is always hard to apply general information to your own situation. That is the gift of this book: real questions from real people in their own words, and the messy situations of ordinary life that do not always lend themselves to clear, academic answers. You will see that the Companions often advise questioners to consult a priest at their local parish so he can offer more detail than is possible on a Web site posting.

Catholic Church law follows a civil law tradition rather than the common law tradition well known in the United States. That means that each Judge is charged with applying the law to the particular situation of this couple in this marriage. Canon law is not a law of precedent where one argues what some other Judge did in some other situation going back many years seeking similar issues. Because of that, it is very important that the Tribunal Judges feel certain they have the truth of the matter, which is why there will be testimony from witnesses and, hopefully, the other spouse as well as from the one seeking a declaration of nullity. The best advice is to be as honest as possible and to offer specific facts, not opinions. The Petitioner will not know for sure whether or not there is proof of nullity. That is a decision for the Judges.

The following questions and answers are related to the various circumstances that arise before, during or after marriage cases.

TERMINOLOGY: WHAT IT ALL MEANS

Declaration of Nullity

Q. I KEEP ASKING THE PRIEST AT OUR PARISH ABOUT annulments and annulment cases and he keeps changing the terms on me. Is this not a correct term for a marriage case? *Henry*

R. "ANNULMENT" IS A MISNOMER COMMONLY USED IN English. The word sounds like the Church does something to a valid marriage to make it null. What the Church does is declare the marriage was never valid in the first place because something essential was missing from the moment of consent. "Declaration of nullity" is the better term because it is more correct and canon lawyers try to be precise about such things. You will notice that the word "annulment" has been edited out of the questions in this book. *Sister Faith*

Tribunal

Q. WHAT IS A TRIBUNAL ANYWAY? The Companions keep referring to sending things to or contacting a tribunal. I am Catholic but I didn't go to a

Catholic school and I don't go to Church very much. I want to marry a really beautiful young woman who is way too serious about practicing her faith. I told her that I can just talk with God in prayer and decide that my marriage was not kosher and deserved to be ended. She insists we need Church approval before she will marry me. I don't mean to be disrespectful, but I don't need some Church folks to make decisions for me. Who are those people anyway? Can you help me convince her to just go ahead and marry me in a civil ceremony? *Jerome*

R. A TRIBUNAL IS A CHURCH COURT. THE CATHOLIC CHURCH has such courts to handle situations related to Church law. Most of the working time of tribunal officials is spent dealing with marriage cases (more about that in a minute). "Those people" who work at the tribunal have training in canon law. Each marriage case involves at least one Judge, a Defender of the Bond (who argues for validity of the marriage) and an auditor (a canon law term for case manager, not someone connected with bookkeeping). There may be others involved as well in more complicated cases. Tribunals also handle other Church matters that involve canonical crimes. These kinds of cases involve a Promoter of Justice instead of a Defender of the Bond of marriage as well as at least three Judges and an auditor. The media recently has focused on the scandal of clergy accused of sexually abusing minors. A priest accused of such a crime could be brought to trial before a Church tribunal, which could decide whether or not he should be dismissed from the clerical state (defrocked). A pastor could receive a penalty from a Church trial for misusing parish funds and not consulting the finance council in his parish as is demanded by Church law.

Your question focuses on marriage cases. Marriage is a public act and involves not only you and your former spouse but also the common good. Marriage is not a private agreement between you and the woman you married but a public act regulated by the civil government and, for Catholics, by Church law. Just as a person who ends a civil marriage needs to get a civil divorce or dissolution, so a Catholic cannot end a marriage privately but must ask the Church through the tribunal to evaluate whether or not the union in question was a valid marriage that remains binding for life even if the spouses have chosen to separate.

You describe the woman you intend to marry as someone who really values her faith. It can only help your marriage with her for you to take time to seriously evaluate your previous choices about marriage and to come to terms with the faith she would want to share with you. I hope you will use the time that the processing of your case will take to learn more about the faith you have not been practicing and to explore with this young woman you have come to love whether you will be able to share life values including faith. I will be praying for both of you. *Sister Faith*

Q. IS THERE ANY WAY FOR MY CASE TO BE SENT TO ANOTHER diocese (other than my own) to be judged? *Greta*

R. A CASE MAY BE HEARD IN ONE OF FOUR POSSIBLE TRIBUNALS:
1) The diocese that was also the place of the marriage.
2) The diocese where your former spouse lives.

3) The place where you live, with the consent of the
tribunal where your former spouse lives provided he also
lives within the same bishop's conference (within the
United States for you).
4) The place where the "most proofs" are to be collected,
that is, for example, where most of the witnesses who
will offer testimony live, again, with the consent of the
tribunal where your former spouse lives.

For example, if the place of marriage is Chicago, and you
and your former spouse and all the major witnesses live in
the Chicago diocese, Chicago is the only place the case may
be heard. Another example: If you live in Boston, and your
former spouse lives in Miami, and the wedding took place in
Dallas and all the witnesses live in San Francisco, then there
is a possibility that the case could be heard in Boston,
Miami, Dallas or San Francisco.

The rule about the four ways a tribunal can be
competent to hear a case is canon 1673. These are the only
options, unless the tribunal (not you as the Petitioner) were
to petition Rome for permission from the Signatura (sort of
a supreme court at the Vatican for such matters) to allow
your case to be heard in another diocese for a serious
reason. For example, the tribunal where I work has heard
several cases for employees of another diocese who are well
known by all those serving at their tribunal so Rome has
given permission for those cases to be judged here. Peace,
Father Mike

Lack of Form

Q. CAN YOU CLARIFY WHAT A LACK OF FORM CASE IS?
I started the tribunal process two years ago this month. That
was before I met my current fiancé. My case is still in the
hands of the tribunal and I feel that they are not moving
quickly at all. We want to have a Catholic wedding because
our spirituality is the center of our relationship. However,
the tribunal's delay in moving forward or even giving a
status report is causing us great pain. Is there any way that I
can get them to move faster? I would think two years is
enough time. Thank you for any insight you can share. *Jodi*

R. CATHOLICS ARE REQUIRED TO MARRY IN CATHOLIC
ceremonies, unless they get a dispensation (a special kind of
permission). If a Catholic did not marry in a Catholic
ceremony, and did not receive a dispensation to marry
outside the Church, the marriage lacks canonical form. With
original documents (the baptismal certificate of the Catholic
party, the civil record of the marriage, and the civil record of
the ending of the marriage) the declaration of nullity is
granted.

I would suspect that this does not fit the description of
your wedding, since you have already progressed to a
tribunal. Typically, Lack of Form cases are very efficient and
quite easy to conclude. You do have the right to contact the
tribunal and ask for an update on your case. Such a request
should be made in writing. I'll keep you and your fiancé in
my prayers. Peace, *Father Mike*

Q. IF A MARRIAGE IS INVALID DUE TO LACK OF CANONICAL form, why is it necessary to declare the marriage null? This I cannot understand. Why does a formal document matter so much if the reason for invalidity speaks for itself? *Mary Grace*

R. IT MAY SEEM EVIDENT TO YOU THAT A MARRIAGE IS INVALID due to lack of form but you might not know all the laws involved. For example, a Catholic could have obtained a dispensation from canonical form allowing her to marry before a Protestant minister with no priest present if, for example, that minister is the father of the groom and the Catholic Church approved him as the official witness. A Lack of Form case usually takes only a few weeks for the tribunal to verify the facts that this was a validly baptized Roman Catholic married without proper canonical form. *Sister Faith*

Q. I AM A CATHOLIC, BUT WAS MARRIED BY A JUSTICE OF THE Peace. What kind of case do I have? I married my husband nine years ago. I was pregnant at the time of our wedding and a Justice of the Peace married us. My husband was married previously and divorced from his first marriage after less than two years. He was not married in the Church. We are both baptized Catholics, and I was confirmed also. Our daughter is baptized in the Church. I was ignorant of the fact that I should not participate in the sacraments until a pilgrimage to Medjugorje several years after our wedding. I would like my marriage to be recognized by the Church and hope you can help guide me in what to do. Thank you for any help you can provide. *Michelle*

R. WHAT YOU HAVE IS A LACK OF FORM CASE. YOU SAY BOTH you and your current spouse are Catholic. He was married before you but that wedding was not according to the rules of the Catholic Church. That means he needs to ask to have his first marriage declared null due to lack of canonical form. For that process, he will need to submit a legal copy of the marriage application or at least the certificate indicating where, when and to whom he was married as well as the name of the Catholic Church where he was baptized so the pastoral minister assisting him can request a baptismal certificate for him. This is a very easy process and usually takes no more than a few weeks to finalize since all is proven in those documents as long as your current civil spouse did not leave the Catholic Church by a formal act (such as being baptized or confirmed or ordained in another religion and if the first wedding was after 1983).

Once the lack of proper canonical form is declared, you and your current spouse will be able to prepare for and celebrate your marriage by making a new act of consent (convalidation) according to the rules of the Catholic Church—before a priest or a deacon and two witnesses, not necessarily a large public ceremony. You are blessed that yours is a relatively simple situation to straighten out. *Sister Faith*

Q. I AM A DIVORCED CATHOLIC. I WAS NOT MARRIED IN THE Catholic Church, but in a nondenominational ceremony. Do I need a declaration of nullity before I get married? *Larry*

R. IF YOU DID NOT ASK FOR AND RECEIVE THE PERMISSION OF the Catholic bishop when you had the marriage ceremony in a nondenominational Christian church, you may re-establish your freedom for marriage in the Catholic Church by requesting a declaration of nullity due to a lack of canonical form.

This is technical language but most parish priests are aware of the procedure. To apply, secure a copy of your civil record of marriage (not the license but the record of marriage), a current copy of your baptismal certificate "with all notations" and a copy of your divorce or dissolution papers to demonstrate that the civil proceedings are completed. You will need to submit these items to the diocesan tribunal who may also have a short questionnaire for you to complete. If you did have the bishop's permission prior to your wedding, you will most likely have to go through a Formal case. *Father Francis*

Ligamen Case

Q. WHAT IF I CAN'T GET ALL THE INFORMATION I NEED? My first husband, whom I divorced, had two previous marriages before me. Was our marriage even valid? I am in the process of presenting a case for this marriage, so that I may remarry in the Catholic Church. I am not Catholic but my fiancé is. As I said before, my ex-husband had two previous marriages before he married me. I have managed to track down both marriage records and divorce records. I also have the court documentation regarding our marriage and divorce. However, my ex-husband has not been cooperative. He will not give me any information regarding his ex-spouses. He would not even tell me the last name of spouse number one. I have tried to contact spouse number two based on the area she lived in and her maiden name and also her parents' names. I am trying to find out information regarding her baptismal status. My ex-husband has been in contact with her but states that she wants no contact from me. He said that he asked her if she was baptized and she says she was but could not remember when or where exactly.

What do I need to do now? I cannot track down wife number one to ask her the same question. She was supposedly Pentecostal. Can I turn in the information I have to the tribunal or will they not even look at it if it is not complete? My ex-husband will not cooperate with the process and I do not know what to do next. I have already spent considerable time and am anxious to get the process started with the tribunal. I am planning to marry next spring and we would like to begin the marriage preparation classes and reserve a date in the parish church. *Sandra*

R. SOUNDS LIKE YOU HAVE A LIGAMEN SITUATION. YOUR former husband was still bound to a previous marriage when he married you. This makes your marriage to him invalid. That is called a documentary case because the facts can be proven from documents for the most part. You already have critical evidence with the marriage records and divorce decrees. It is important to see if there is any reason to suspect either of his previous wives were Roman Catholic and married out of the Church but you already know that from what you have. Ask the pastoral minister working with you to send what you have to the tribunal to see if there is enough evidence to render a decision. Sounds to me like there is. Good luck. *Sister Faith*

Q. MY GIRLFRIEND (A NON-CATHOLIC) WAS PREVIOUSLY married to a man who was divorced. My question is, does she need to present a marriage case since her first marriage was not valid? *Dan*

R. YOUR GIRLFRIEND WILL NEED TO PRESENT WHAT IS CALLED A Ligamen case. This involves an investigation to be sure the previous marriage for her ex-husband was his first marriage and that he was not a Catholic marrying without proper canonical form, either of which could have made his first marriage an invalid one. If he were bound to his first marriage, his attempt at marriage with your girlfriend would then have been invalid due to the prior bond of his first marriage, which is called a Ligamen case in Church law terms. I presume you are a Catholic who is trying to find out if you could be free to marry your girlfriend sometime in the future. Take her to meet with a priest at a parish you know to talk about beginning a Ligamen case to determine if she can be free to marry you in the Church. God's blessings on your journey together. *Sister Faith*

Pauline Privilege and the Favor of the Faith
Q. DID THE CATHOLIC CHURCH MAKE THE PROCEDURES known as the Pauline Privilege with the following Biblical

verse in mind? In 1 Corinthians 7:13-15, Paul instructs the
believer not to send away the unbelieving mate; but if the
unbeliever chooses to leave (divorce) then the believer is to
tell the mate to go. The believer is not under bondage in
this case. *Virginia*

R. THE PASSAGE YOU REFER TO IS THE BASIS FOR A PAULINE
Privilege, which is sought when two unbaptized people
marry and then divorce. When there is one baptized party, it
is called a Favor of the Faith (sometimes previously called a
Privilege of Faith). Peace, *Father Mike*

Q. AM I ELIGIBLE FOR A FAVOR OF THE FAITH OR A PAULINE
Privilege case? Neither my present husband nor myself have
ever been baptized Christian. Neither one of us had ever
attended church nor was married in a church. My ex-husband
had been baptized as a teenager but we didn't marry in a
church and never attended church while we were married.
My present husband and his ex-wife were not married in a
church and his ex-wife had also never been baptized.
If neither of us had ever been baptized, then might we be
able to apply for a Pauline Privilege? If my first husband was
baptized would I be eligible? If my current husband and his
first wife were never baptized, then could he apply for this
privilege? *Carole*

R. WHATEVER PRIVILEGE APPLIES TO YOUR SITUATION DEPENDS
on the baptismal status of each spouse. This refers to each
of you and each of your former spouses, not you and your

intended spouse. Since you tell me that neither your intended spouse nor his first wife were ever baptized Christian, he could apply for a Pauline Privilege provided she is still not baptized and he is seeking baptism. Since your former spouse was baptized but you were not, you could apply for a Favor of the Faith case provided the failure of the marriage was not your fault. Both never baptized = Pauline Privilege. One never baptized = Favor of the Faith. Hope this helps you. *Sister Faith*

Q. IF AN UNBAPTIZED, DIVORCED PERSON WANTS TO BECOME Catholic, why then is their previous marriage not declared invalid also since they were not married in the Catholic Church? *Charlie*

R. IF SOMEONE IS UNBAPTIZED, DIVORCED AND MIGHT WANT to marry again and/or become a Catholic, he or she may petition the tribunal. The tribunal will then instruct the parties to either seek the Pauline Privilege (if both parties were unbaptized at the time of the wedding, the non-baptism of both can be proven and one remains non-baptized) or the Favor of the Faith (if it can be proven that at least one of the parties was unbaptized at the time of the wedding and the petitioner was not the culpable cause for the marriage ending). They may also present what the marriage tribunal calls Formal cases, where the validity of their consent is examined. *Father Mike*

Defender of the Bond

Q. WHO IS THE DEFENDER OF THE BOND? MY FIANCÉ IS IN the Army and we are seeking a declaration of nullity for his previous marriage through the archdiocese that serves the military. We started the process over a year ago and plan to marry before moving overseas. All of our paperwork is completed, witnesses have responded and he paid the fee. He sent a letter to them last week asking for an estimate of time until we receive our final judgment and he received a letter back from the tribunal saying, "Your case is in line for review going to the Defender." What does that mean? How much longer? *Katherine*

R. WORKING ON EVERY MARRIAGE CASE WILL BE ONE TO THREE Judges and a Defender of the Bond whose job it is to argue for the validity of the marriage if there is evidence indicating this was a valid marriage that cannot be declared null. There is a Defender of the Bond in first instance (the local tribunal) and second instance (the court of appeal). Usually the Defender would write a formal brief about the case before it goes to the Judge(s) for decision.

If the letter your intended spouse received came from the first tribunal to hear this case, it means the case will soon be with a Judge for the decision. If the marriage is declared null in first instance, it must, by law, go on to an Appeal Court that usually will hear the case within three months. Only if both courts agree that the marriage is null will your intended spouse be free to marry you. Please ask your intended spouse to ask the priest who helped him present his case to explain the timing in his particular diocese. *Sister Faith*

MARRIAGE CASES: CANONICAL, NOT BIBLICAL HISTORY

Q. WHERE IN THE BIBLE DOES IT SAY THAT THE CHURCH CAN grant a declaration of nullity and that just asking God for forgiveness is not enough? Can you give me Scripture that explains this? *Ami*

R. A DECLARATION OF NULLITY IS A LEGAL STATEMENT BY THE Catholic Church, which says that the Church holds persons either free of or bound to a marriage that they entered into in the past. It is not based on the Bible but on the Church's historical experience. In Matthew, Chapter 19 and Mark, Chapter 10, Jesus says that marriage is forever and spouses should not divorce. Even in Jesus' time, people did divorce. After Jesus ascended into heaven, people kept divorcing and coming to the Church. You can give people the Gospel passages, but they will tell you that Jesus did not intend His teachings for them in their particular circumstance, and that they are right to divorce.

Why is not just asking God's forgiveness enough? Why have people for all these years come to the Church for recognition of their new marriages? Marriage is not just something between two persons. It involves two or more families, a parish community, and a church. I believe the tribunal process exists because people want others to agree with what they did and are doing. *Father Francis*

EVERY CASE IS A "POSSIBLE" CASE

Q. WHY WON'T MY PRIEST LET ME BEGIN THE MARRIAGE CASE process? I am a divorced and remarried Catholic and my parish priest told me prior to my remarriage that marriage is for life and that I could not expect to be granted a declaration of nullity. I did not apply for one and I have been suffering without my faith for six years. My ex-husband, who emotionally abused me through adultery for fourteen years, ended my former marriage. He finally left me and went to live with another woman. I sought counseling from three separate counselors. I was willing to continue the marriage, but he refused. I can't believe I must be penalized by being unworthy of the sacraments after all that I went through. My present husband is a Catholic, but he has not practiced his faith since his teens. Is there any way to seek a declaration of nullity after all this time, and what happens to the status of this marriage? *Lisa*

R. EVERY SPOUSE WHOSE MARRIAGE ENDS IN CIVIL DIVORCE OR dissolution has the right to petition a tribunal of the Catholic Church in order to re-establish his or her freedom for a new marriage. Even after many years as a canon lawyer, I continue to be amazed at the number of people who ask nonprofessional people to answer technical questions and then follow that advice. Whether or not the petition is successful depends upon the facts that can be gathered as well as the Church's jurisprudence and procedures. Most parish priests today have some knowledge of canon law, but many are not able to advise people in this area. If your parish priest cannot assist you, call the diocesan tribunal and speak with someone there who can advise you both about your first marriage and the present one. *Father Francis*

VARIOUS GROUNDS FOR NULLITY

Q. PLEASE EXPLAIN WHAT "GROUNDS" FOR NULLITY MEANS. Who determines these "grounds?" At the time of our filing our paperwork, nothing was said about the grounds that we'd be filing under. I assumed that when our paperwork got to the archdiocese that they would determine the grounds, which they ultimately did. I don't remember exactly what they were, but, does this mean that after review of our petitions they felt that there were sufficient grounds to proceed with our petitions, or is this just a formality and the reasons don't come out until the case is argued before the tribunal? *Conrad*

R. WHEN A PETITION FOR A FORMAL CASE IS SUBMITTED, YOU are asked why you think your marriage is invalid according to Church law. Often people do not know what that answer might be so the pastoral minister working with them helps them word the reason in canonical (Church) terms.

You mention receiving from the tribunal a statement that named the grounds for nullity. That is the reason for nullity that is being considered in your particular case based on the evidence you have submitted.

If the tribunal found no reason to even question the validity of your marriage, you would have been notified about that. So, now it seems that if what you allege about your marriage can be proven (through documents, witnesses, perhaps the testimony of your former spouse also) then it is possible that an affirmative decision can be reached. *Sister Faith*

Q. CAN YOU GIVE ME A LIST OF VALID REASONS ONE MIGHT use when seeking a declaration of nullity? *Kathryn*

R. THE REASONS FOR DECLARATION OF NULLITY ARE CALLED "grounds of nullity." In general these pertain to two types of deficiencies in marriage consent. The first is that there was something wrong with the consent itself. For example, a very young lady might become pregnant and believe that she has to marry, or maybe, her father or mother "demand" that she marry. Another example might be that someone intends to marry another but also intends to divorce if that marriage should not work out.

Another type of ground looks at the person and their "capacity" to enter and sustain marriage as a partnership of life and love. Someone suffering from drug addiction, or some sorts of psychological problems might not be able to stay married.

If I might offer a suggestion, I have found that it is often easier to work with professional canonists. Tell them the whole story and let them try to figure out the grounds of possible nullity for you. Some cases can become a bit complicated when the grounds argued before a court or tribunal can require specific proofs. *Father Francis*

GRAVE LACK OF DUE DISCRETION AND NULLITY

Q. WHAT DO THE GROUNDS "GRAVE LACK OF DUE DISCRETION for marriage" mean in lay terms? I have just received my formal petition from the tribunal to sign and send back regarding a case about the validity of my previous marriage. The canonical grounds read: grave lack of due discretion for marriage. Thank you. *Carole*

R. THERE ARE CERTAIN CRITERIA REQUIRED FOR "DISCRETION necessary to marry." The discretion of judgment needed to marry validly involves:

- An understanding of the essential obligations of Christian marriage, at least in substance;
- A mature evaluation of the relationship;
- A free choice of the will.

In other words, you have to know about the responsibilities of marriage, critically evaluate your relationship with this person in these circumstances, and then be able to make a free choice. You'll be in my prayers. *Father Mike*

Q. I WAS NOT IN THE RIGHT STATE OF MIND WHEN I AGREED to get married and once I realized how brainwashed I was I got out of it because it was not real. Are these grounds for nullity? At the age of fifteen I joined a nondenominational "church" on my own, which I liked. I did not have a good home life and I wanted something that made me happy. I joined the church of the boy I was dating at the time. Also at that young age, still fifteen, another church member told me that it was God's will for me to marry this boy I was dating. The boy also believed this and told me so. I honestly believe I was looking for love and acceptance from somewhere and anywhere so I believed anything this young man told me.

I married him two days after my eighteenth birthday because that is what he wanted, and he was the man in the relationship. I was taught in this church that the man was in control of the relationship. He was controlling and the church was controlling. I came to my senses after a long time and left that church, and then after trying hard to save it I realized my marriage was a sham too, so I ended it. The church has closed down since that time. I was married to him for three years before we split up.

I started attending a Lutheran church after we separated. This is the only church where I felt comfortable. The pastor there welcomed me. I am now engaged to a wonderful man who is Catholic. We were told that I need to present a marriage case so he can marry me. From what I have told you, do you think there is much of a chance that I will get an affirmative decision? After thinking about what this requires, I have realized I do not think my marriage was even real. Thank you. *Angie*

R. FROM THE INFORMATION YOU HAVE PROVIDED, I BELIEVE you may well have a sound case to present to a tribunal for a declaration of nullity. And I am pleased the Lutheran pastor has welcomed you and provided a community where you can worship. In order to marry your Catholic fiancé, you will need to present a marriage case. Explain your situation as honestly as you can. Cases take time, so do not delay beginning yours. Once a declaration of nullity is granted you will be free to marry in the Catholic Church or with permission from the Catholic Church in a ceremony at the Lutheran Church where you worship. Good luck to both of you. *Father Francis*

Q. DOESN'T A PERSON HAVE TO DESIRE TO BE TRULY MARRIED for it to be valid? Doesn't the deception that initiated this marriage make it invalid? Don't the parties who are to be married have to enter marriage in love and loving each other for it to be valid? I am writing because I recently decided to join the Catholic Church after a long-overdue faith journey. I am involved in a previous marriage that ended in divorce.

My concerns are these: we both were sixteen when we got married by her father, a Pentecostal minister. I never desired to marry her for the reasons of matrimony. I was in an abusive home from age seven and I received constant abuse from my stepfather. Something just clicked in high school, and I came up with the idea that marrying this girl who was almost a stranger would free me from my home and the abuse. Well, it did do that and saved me all the hardships of being a sixteen-year-old on my own.

The girl was sixteen as well and I never was in love with her. I can't see how she was in love with me either since she had a similar situation in her home, as it turned out.

Anyway, we lied to our parents about the reason we were to be married so that they would sign the consent. We told them that she was pregnant but she was not. We were married for less than five years, and she began to want to see other men and was unfaithful to me. Once I found out from her about the infidelity, she moved out and I filed for divorce. Thank you for reading this and for your answer.
David

R. IT IS VERY DIFFICULT, ALMOST IMPOSSIBLE, FOR TEENAGERS who come from abusive situations to be able to enter into a valid marriage with those elements. In Catholic teaching, marriage is a partnership of life and love whereby two people make the following qualities part of the relationship: Self-revelation, the ability to tell the other person what is really going on inside of yourself; understanding, being able to understand who you are as an individual and as a couple; and caring or loving, which is the ability to sacrifice and put the good of the other before yourself.

I wish you well and encourage you to work with those who can help you heal the past so that no previous problems influence a new marriage. *Father Mike*

LACK OF LOVE AND NULLITY

Q. MY FRIEND WOULD LIKE TO HAVE HIS MARRIAGE DECLARED null. His wife has told him that she never should have married him because she never loved him—the same thing she told him three months before they got married, but he convinced her that she just had "cold feet" and they went through the marriage anyway. Is this a ground for nullity? We are both Catholic and have developed a wonderful friendship over the last six months. We would like to start dating as soon as the divorce is final. And we would even like to get married. *Ellen*

R. ACCORDING TO THE LAW OF THE CHURCH, CONSENT MAKES marriage. Consent can be measured (for example, the couple exchanged their vows on this date, in this church, etc., and they are married). Love can't be measured. And all of us love imperfectly. But love is an important aspect of marriage.

Once the divorce is finalized, if he chooses, he can seek a declaration of nullity. Even though "she didn't love me" is not a ground to declare a marriage null, it may point to something that was missing at the time of consent that is essential to marriage, as the Catholic Church understands marriage. And if she participates in the process, the tribunal will have a fuller understanding of the relationship in arriving at their decision.

I hope this helps. I would encourage you to consider moving slowly in your relationship with him because second marriages fail at a higher rate than first marriages. May God bless you and those you love. Please write again if we might be able to assist. *Father Mike*

INFIDELITY AND NULLITY

Q. DOES INFIDELITY PRIOR TO A MARRIAGE MAKE A MARRIAGE invalid? I am a Catholic and so is my fiancé. He was married in the Church and is now divorced.

One of the underlying problems in his marriage was that his ex-wife lied to him about her fidelity prior to the marriage. While they were dating she had been "dating" others (he wasn't). About two years (I think) after the wedding, she told him about this. He was understandably very upset and felt betrayed. He never really got over it and says he never would have married her had he known.

He was married a long time, about ten years, but I know from conversations having nothing to do with whether the marriage was valid, that this lie festered and in many ways contributed to and/or caused the problems that ended their marriage.

If it is possible to have the marriage declared null, will it be necessary to have his ex-wife involved in the process? They don't have the best of relationships (obviously), and they have two children together. He does not want to cause any more problems with her than necessary, to keep the relationship stable for the children. Thank you, *Eloise*

R. IT IS VERY UNLIKELY THAT YOUR INTENDED SPOUSE WILL BE able to prove that his first wife never intended to be faithful to him, which would be a reason for nullity. The fact of infidelity is not such a reason. Also, the respondent (the other spouse) has a right to be notified about the process but need not participate in it. That is her choice. The case will only be helped to come to a decision if she chooses to participate.

Just advise your intended spouse to be as honest as he can while offering specific facts and not opinions about himself and the marriage. The tribunal will determine if there is a reason why the marriage can be declared null or not. There is no way to know in the beginning of the process whether the decision will be affirmative or negative. He just needs to be honest and put the results in God's hands. *Sister Faith*

Intention against Children and Nullity

Q. When I married my husband, I wanted children and he said he did not. He has since then divorced me, and has children with his new wife. How can I prove he never wanted children? Do you think I have a case?

My ex-husband and I were married for only a few years. During pre-Cana he said he did not want children and that was documented in the notes. I said I did want children. The priest who married us said everything was fine but we needed to work on the children issue down the road. Afterward my husband was unfaithful, divorced me and is now married with two children with his new wife. I want to try to get a declaration of nullity but based on what I am hearing I am not sure I can do it. I go to Mass every Sunday and I would like to remarry in the Church. Some people have told me that because my ex-husband now has children it is going to be tough to prove to a tribunal he did not want them with me. He also told everyone I am the one who refused to have children he wanted. I just don't know what to do. If I present a case will it be negative? I want to do the right thing but I also don't want to be hurt or embarrassed by any of this. It all seems intimidating to me. Please help. Do you think I have a case? Thank you. *Brittany*

R. There are several grounds for a declaration of nullity. An intention against children is one of them. Based on what you have told me, you do have a case. However, the tribunal establishes the grounds to be considered in a case. Meeting with your parish priest to talk about the process may be helpful and make the process seem less intimidating. You could also ask to speak with someone at your tribunal. I work at a tribunal, and I answer questions all day long for people involved in presenting cases.

You are correct that some marriages are not declared invalid. Sometimes this happens due to a lack of evidence. At the tribunal where I serve, we encourage people to present a case. That is the only way to determine if there is a reason why the marriage can be declared invalid or not. God bless! *Father Mike*

Premarital Pregnancy and Nullity

Q. How much weight will the fact that I was pregnant at my first wedding play in the decision? I am currently going through the tribunal process. I just handed my final copy to my priest. I am scared to death that I will receive a negative response. I am only thirty, and I would like to marry again. *Laura*

R. A simple answer to your question is that the outcome of a declaration of nullity will depend greatly on how much pressure the fact of your being pregnant influenced your decision to marry at the time. This is a difficult area to evaluate without knowing all the facts of your case. If I were you I would share my fears with the priest who helped you prepare the case. I advise people that I help to keep a positive attitude and pray. All one can do is to tell the story truthfully and the best that they can. It will work out. *Father Francis.*

Substance Abuse and Nullity

Q. I was under the influence of drugs. is this grounds for a declaration of nullity? Can I hope for a declaration of nullity after ten years of marriage and four wonderful kids?

I met my former wife in my teens and married four years later in a haze of substance abuse. We were under the influence of drugs at the wedding. We abused drugs the whole ten years of the marriage. I have turned my life back to God, and I gave up all alcohol and drugs. I went back to court and now have custody of my kids. I now spend every waking moment raising my four children to be Christ-like. They are all now getting good grades. I have reconnected with them and the rewards of my conversion have been beyond my hopes.

Now I have met another woman. She has two children but was never married. She is taking RCIA. If I am to live a Christ-like relationship, I must maintain my being Catholic and present a marriage case before I try to marry her. I am prepared to do whatever it takes. I do not want to start to live an unholy relationship.

I am tired of the fighting with my ex-wife, and this will certainly cause more. Is my decision to pursue a marriage case a sound one? God bless you all! *Thomas*

R. From what you tell us you are Catholic. If you did not have a Catholic wedding, you have a Lack of Form. If you did have a Catholic wedding, you will need to present a Formal case.

Information about your substance abuse during the courtship and marriage will be important evidence for your case since it likely impaired your judgment at the time of consent. There is no time limit after which a marriage cannot be declared null. Do meet with a priest at your parish to talk about what kind of case you need to present. May God bless you especially in your recovery from drug abuse and your attempts to be a good father to your children. *Sister Faith*

COHABITATION AND NULLITY

Q. HOW DOES THE CHURCH VIEW COHABITATION OR premarital sex in regards to marriage cases? Does living together prior to marriage (in a non-Catholic home) give a compelling reason for declaring a marriage null?

I am a non-Catholic wanting to marry a Catholic. I am divorced and understand that I must present a marriage case to see if I can be "free to marry" in the Catholic Church. *Art*

R. COHABITATION BY A COUPLE BEFORE A WEDDING IS NOT conclusive proof that the subsequent marriage was an invalid one but it is evidence about the values of the two parties to this relationship.

The Catholic Church teaches that sexual intimacy outside the bond of matrimony is sinful. Cohabitation usually implies a sexual relationship, which I presume you mean in your question. Apart from Church teaching, there is also the sociological evidence that a divorce is more likely when there has been cohabitation before the wedding than when there has not. Just be as honest as you can in describing all aspects of your relationship during the tribunal process. God bless your efforts. *Sister Faith*

INFERTILITY AND NULLITY

Q. MY EX-WIFE HAD A TUBAL LIGATION SOME YEARS BEFORE our wedding; I was fully aware that she had this procedure and that we would have no children together. Should I take this to mean that I have an open and shut case for nullity? I am a divorced Catholic and am starting the process of seeking a declaration of nullity. According to canon 1101, section 2 (parentheses mine), "If, however either (my ex-wife) or both of the parties should by a positive act of will (sterilization) exclude marriage itself or any essential element of marriage (having children) or any essential property, such party contracts invalidly." *David*

R. IN YOUR CASE, THE TUBAL LIGATION IS NOT A REASON YOUR marriage was invalid. You knew about this and chose to marry her anyway. The obligation in marriage is not to actually have a child (as you know many couples long for a child and are unable to have one even though they use no artificial means to prevent conception) but to be open to having a child, to exchange the right to offspring from a loving union.

If your spouse had a tubal ligation before the wedding and did not tell you about it in order to exclude children from your union or perhaps knowing you would not have married her if you knew she could not conceive, that could be a reason for your marriage to be declared null. I hope this answers your questions. *Sister Faith*

Q. WHAT IF THE WOMAN HAS A TUBAL LIGATION DURING THE marriage? Does this invalidate the marriage? *Caroline*

R. THE ACT OF HAVING A TUBAL LIGATION DURING THE marriage would not be invalidating. The reasons behind having the tubal ligation may point to invalidity. For example, a woman on the day of her wedding knowingly intends not to have children during her marriage, but does not reveal this to the spouse. Two years into the marriage, her husband wants to have a child. She decides to have the tubal ligation in order to avoid pregnancy and motherhood. Later, citing stresses in the relationship, they divorce. These facts may indicate she had an intention against children at the time of the wedding that may lead to a declaration of nullity.

Another example: A woman and her husband have three children. The last pregnancy is especially difficult, and the mother nearly loses her life. She and her husband decide she will have a tubal ligation. Later, citing stresses in the relationship, they divorce. These facts probably would not lead to a declaration of nullity.

Both examples have a tubal ligation involved. Each decision made by a marriage tribunal applies the law to the facts of a specific case. From my experience at the tribunal where I serve, there are no automatic decisions where a tubal ligation is involved. *Father Mike*

NON-CATHOLICS REQUIRE DECLARATIONS OF NULLITY TOO

Q. WHY SHOULD NON-CATHOLICS BE REQUIRED TO PRESENT a marriage case if they were not married in the Church? While I agree that Catholics need to abide by the rules of the Catholic Church, I do not understand why non-Catholics should. So many Catholics writing in are married to non-Catholics who have been divorced. I would think that the Church would be eager to have Catholics return to the Church, especially when they would be bringing their children with them. *Kellie*

R. THE CATHOLIC CHURCH'S LAWS DEALING WITH MARRIAGE bind Catholics. It's not the non-Catholic who is bound to follow the law of the Church, but the Catholic party. But, obviously, this affects a non-Catholic who needs a declaration of nullity in order to marry a Catholic.

The Church's teaching on divorce and remarriage is based on Jesus' teaching about divorce and remarriage. Jesus did not differentiate between baptized and unbaptized, believer or nonbeliever. That's why a non-Catholic must seek a declaration of nullity or dissolution of a prior marriage if he or she is seeking to marry a Catholic who is free to marry.

In my work at the tribunal, I have learned that there are some Protestant denominations in which the minister will not preside at a wedding ceremony if one of the parties has been married before and the former spouse is still alive.

A Catholic who has married a divorced person is still encouraged to attend Mass, but they may not receive Holy Communion. *Father Mike*

Q. WHAT IF YOU HAVE TWO NON-CATHOLICS WHO HAVE BEEN divorced and marry one another who want to join the Catholic faith? I always see references to one non-Catholic and one Catholic wanting to marry. If both non-Catholics have never been baptized and want to join the Catholic Church, I understand that they have to have their previous marriages declared null by the tribunal. Don't you have situations of someone wanting to become Catholic who wasn't born Catholic or isn't planning on marrying a Catholic who has been married and divorced previously who have been successful in becoming members of the Catholic faith? *Conrad*

R. YOU ARE CORRECT THAT BOTH OF YOU WILL NEED TO HAVE your previous marriages declared null or dissolved through a Pauline Privilege or Favor of the Faith before you can become Catholic.

There are many situations of two unbaptized people who are married to each other choosing to both become Catholic. Such situations do not show up in questions on this site unless the question is about a previous marriage for one of them or in your case both of you.

If you and your previous spouse (or she and her previous spouse) were both not baptized and the former spouse remains unbaptized now and is not planning to become baptized, see the explanations about Pauline Privilege elsewhere in this book. God's blessings on your conversion. *Sister Faith*

Q. DOES MY NON-CATHOLIC, ONCE-DIVORCED FIANCÉ NEED TO present a case before he marries me?

My fiancé and I are in a bind. He was married before. He is non-Catholic and a Justice of the Peace in a nonreligious ceremony married him. We keep getting contradictory answers about whether or not he needs to present a marriage case. Some say no because it was not a religious service. *Katy*

R. THE ANSWER TO YOUR QUESTION IS "YES." YOUR FIANCÉ needs to approach the Church through presenting a tribunal case to determine if he is free to marry you in the Catholic Church. The Catholic Church upholds the validity of all first marriages and considers them to be binding for life unless invalidity is proven. Non-Catholics are not required to marry in a religious ceremony for their marriages to be valid. However, there are many ways the marriage may not have been valid, and contacting the tribunal might help him determine this. Good luck and God bless. *Father Francis.*

Q. IS THERE A WAY MY FORMERLY DIVORCED NON-CATHOLIC wife can still present a marriage case even though we are already married civilly? Is there a way I can make things right between me and the Church?

I am Catholic; my wife is not. She is divorced. I ignored that when we married outside the Church, and I was not taking my faith seriously. Now I realize how important it is to me to have my marriage recognized and be able to raise any children we may have as Catholics. *John*

R. YES, VERY DEFINITELY. IT IS POSSIBLE FOR YOUR CIVIL SPOUSE to present a marriage case to a Catholic tribunal. Begin by introducing her to a priest at the parish you attend or someone else who handles marriage cases for that parish. She will need to gather the civil marriage license, certificate, divorce/dissolution decree and baptismal certificate if she has one. There will be questions to answer, and it takes time so encourage her to stay with the process and not become discouraged. If her marriage is declared null, then you will both be ready to meet with a priest about marrying in the Church—a convalidation. Good luck to both of you.
Father Francis

Q. WHAT STEPS WOULD I NEED TO FULFILL TO HAVE FULL acceptance in the Catholic Church and for a potential marriage to be fully recognized by the Catholic Church with all the benefits of full recognition (i.e., both of us being able to receive Holy Communion)? I am in a relationship with a woman who is Catholic and free to marry. I am divorced with two kids and am a Methodist. I am interested and willing to become Catholic. *Edgar*

R. THERE ARE TWO THINGS AT ISSUE HERE—THE NEED FOR A declaration of nullity and becoming a Catholic. Before a

Catholic woman may marry you, your first marriage would have to be declared null by a Catholic tribunal (whether or not you become Catholic yourself). Please meet with a priest at the parish where you hope to marry to find out what you need to do to present a case.

To become Catholic, you will need to go through a process of incorporation and information which is called the Rite of Christian Initiation for Adults (RCIA). Again, check with the parish where you hope to marry about their program and what you need to do to begin preparation. Welcome to the Church. *Sister Faith*

MULTIPLE CASES

Q. I HAVE BEEN MARRIED THREE TIMES; WHAT DO I DO?
I am writing here because I am too embarrassed to go to my priest. I have made mistakes in my life. I have had three marriages, all of which failed. I have come back to the Church now and I would very much like to have the marriages declared null but I don't know if my efforts would be futile. My first marriage was at the age of twenty to a non-Catholic man. A priest married us in the Church. It only lasted three years. My second marriage was in a courthouse (no church) and that lasted ten years. My third marriage lasted only five years, again not in a church. Do I try to get my first marriage declared null? And are my other marriages valid and do I need to do anything about them? May I receive Holy Communion? Thank you for your help.
Rosemary

R. IF YOU ARE CURRENTLY LIVING A CHASTE LIFE AS A DIVORCED person you are free to share fully in the sacramental life of the Catholic Church if you have not committed any grave sins. But I would suggest that you receive the sacrament of reconciliation. It is truly a sacrament of healing.

If you are planning to remarry, or there is the possibility of remarriage in the future, you should seek declarations of nullity. Based on what you have written, you would need to present what is known as a Formal case for your first marriage. Because your second and third marriages were outside the Church, you can present these as Lack of Form cases since you, as a Catholic, did not marry in front of a priest or a deacon with two witnesses. Since your second and third marriages lack canonical form, they are invalid by that fact. My God bless you richly! Peace, *Father Mike*

Q. IF MY FIRST MARRIAGE IS DECLARED NULL, CAN I RETURN to the sacraments, or does my present marriage to a non-Catholic preclude this? I was a Protestant and married a Catholic outside the Church. Within several years, I converted to Catholicism, and the Church recognized our marriage as a valid Catholic marriage. Unfortunately, our marriage failed several years later, and we divorced but never had the marriage declared null. I remarried a non-Catholic (again outside the Church), a woman who has no intention of changing her faith. *Jared*

R. YOUR PRESENT LEGAL STATUS IN THE CATHOLIC CHURCH IS that of a divorced Catholic who is in an irregular marriage.

In order to return to the sacraments, you need to re-establish your freedom for marriage through the tribunal process. If you are successful in doing that, and if your second wife is free to marry as understood in Catholic teaching, you can convalidate your present civil union. I would urge you to seek some canonical help in your parish or diocese.
Father Francis

WITNESSES AND RESPONDENTS

Q. IF I PRESENT A MARRIAGE CASE, WHO ARE THE WITNESSES to be called on? What if my ex-wife does not want the marriage declared null? *Jim*

R. WITNESSES WOULD BE PEOPLE YOU NAME AS KNOWING YOU or something about your marriage firsthand. Your former spouse also has the right to name witnesses. Your former spouse does not need to take part in the process and does not need to agree to it. She must be notified the case is happening, and she must be offered the chance to give testimony herself if she chooses to do that. I hope you will meet with someone from a parish near you to begin the process. *Sister Faith*

Q. ARE THERE ANY RESTRICTIONS ON WHO I CAN OR CANNOT ask to be my witnesses? For example, are family members not allowed to serve as witnesses? I will be initiating the process of presenting a marriage case in the next month, once my divorce decree is final. *Roger*

R. YES, FAMILY MEMBERS MAY BE WITNESSES. THE MORE THEY saw you in person during the courtship and marriage, the better witnesses they will be because they have their own observations and are not just able to say what you told them at the time.

The best witnesses are those who knew both of you during the courtship and early marriage since it is the time of consent that is in question in a marriage case. If there are no witnesses who knew both of you, someone who knew you well would be helpful.

Do consider members of the wedding party who are usually chosen because they are close to you at the time. Do not list your children as witnesses since they know nothing about the time of consent, which is in question, and it is awkward to ask a child to evaluate the relationship of the parents. An exception to this would be adult children from a previous marriage who knew you both during the courtship.

May God bless you in your search for truth about your previous marriage. *Sister Faith*

Q. DOES THE CHURCH HAVE TO INVOLVE MY FORMER SPOUSE? What if she opposes my petition? *Jim*

R. IF YOUR FORMER SPOUSE IS OPPOSED TO THE WHOLE process, she is free to state that when contacted by the tribunal. The tribunal is required by Church law to contact her. Her testimony may support the validity of the marriage or her testimony may support the invalidity of the marriage. Every case is different.

With every marriage case, the tribunal tries to determine if the consent by each of the parties on their wedding day was valid. If the consent of one or both of the parties was invalid according to the laws and teaching of the Catholic Church, then a declaration of nullity is granted. Something must be missing from the beginning of the marriage. Once again, every case is different. God's blessings to you!
Father Mike

Q. ARE WITNESSES ESSENTIAL TO A MARRIAGE CASE? IF I, AS the Respondent, don't supply any, do I hurt my position? Is my own testimony enough? *Eric*

R. NOT HAVING WITNESSES IS USUALLY DETRIMENTAL TO A case. But, there are different kinds of cases. In cases processed due to lack of canonical form witnesses are rarely needed. The declaration of nullity is based on documents. For a Formal case, a decision to declare a marriage invalid could not occur with only the testimony of the Petitioner who is seeking the declaration of nullity. The facts in the Petitioner's testimony need to be corroborated. The allegations must be proven. The corroboration, the proof, usually comes from witnesses, documents and the other spouse. Also, canon 1573 states that the deposition of a single witness cannot constitute full proof unless the witness is acting in some sort of official capacity. *Father Mike*

Q. WHAT DOES IT MEAN WHEN THE TRIBUNAL "CLOSES THE Acts of the case?" Can I supply witnesses still? I was thinking of contacting a counselor I saw at the time. The letter I received from the tribunal read, "I will again suggest that if you wish to uphold the validity of your marriage, the validity that the Church believes at the present time is in question, I suggest you notify me in writing that you wish to present witnesses."

This sounds to me like a decision has been made unless I can prove (through witnesses) otherwise. Why isn't my testimony enough? My ex-wife was a Jekyll and Hyde. She presented one face to our friends and family and I lived with another face. So anyone observing the marriage would side with her story. *Eric*

R. THE TRIBUNAL IS TELLING YOU THAT THE LAW PRESUMES every marriage is valid unless the opposite is proved to be true. They are saying that the Petitioner, your former spouse, has submitted witnesses who corroborate what she has said about reasons why your marriage might have been invalid. They are asking if you would like to present witnesses who might offer a different perspective. Certainly, a counselor you saw would be an excellent and more objective witness. You could also name others who knew you and/or knew your former spouse. I hope you will offer some witnesses to help the tribunal officials get to the truth about your marriage. *Sister Faith*

Q. Can I get a declaration of nullity without
witnesses or even knowing where my former spouse is?
And can somebody help with finding her if we have to? My
wife and I wish to be married in the Catholic Church. She is
Catholic. I am not. I understand the need for and agree with
getting my first marriage declared null. I have a question
regarding witnesses. My previous marriage happened
nineteen years ago and I have not seen or talked to my ex-
spouse for over thirteen years. I don't know her address or
where she might be. Also, there isn't anybody who can be a
witness to our marriage. I was in the Navy and married this
person because she got pregnant, although later the child
turned out not to be mine. I just wanted to do the right
thing at the time. I didn't love her. My parents did not meet
her until months after we were married, maybe even more
than a year. I have no other witnesses either, because at the
time, many of my shipmates were not even aware of my
marriage. Since I have been discharged from the Navy, I have
had no contact with any of the people I knew at the time.

My wife, whom I love dearly, wants desperately to rejoin
her Church and raise our children in the Catholic faith.
Please help. Any help you can give will be very appreciated.
Mark

R. In recent years, the Holy See has been most insistent
on contacting the former spouse. But have faith, your
situation is not as unique as it may seem. I have investigated
similar cases over the past years. Basically, not being able to
contact your ex-wife or any witnesses is like asking a fighter

to go into the ring with both hands tied behind his back. In regards to witness testimony, Judges determine the number and quality of witnesses. Your tribunal will likely have a list of Web sites that may help you locate your former spouse and/or witnesses. I really think that you need an experienced canonist to sit down and work through the facts of your case with you. Your diocese should have someone who will talk with you. Good luck and do not give up. *Father Francis*

Q. WHY DOES THE TRIBUNAL NEED MY ABUSIVE EX-HUSBAND'S testimony to conduct my marriage case? To return to the Church, I was told by a nun that I had to go through the tribunal process. That was fine with me until I was told that I had to try to find an address for my ex-spouse, and he would be contacted. He was abusive. I understand the dynamics of why I became involved in the first place. I am a recovering alcoholic and have many years in AA. I was married to an alcoholic for only six months years ago. I later married a wonderful non-Catholic out of the Church. I have recovered and worked through many issues. I was also told that I needed witnesses. I could get letters from professionals that I have worked with to try to become a better person. I am sure they could tell you that I have come a long way.

I told the nun that I was afraid of contacting my ex-spouse or old friends about this, and she asked if I have had therapy so my fears of my former spouse will no longer control me. I did not like her asking that. I was looking forward to getting the spiritual part of my life together. I just am not at ease with this process. I am not asking you to do anything really, just thanks for listening. *Sally*

R. I HEAR YOUR FRUSTRATION AND ALSO YOUR LONGING TO come back to the Church. If you present your marriage case in the diocese where you were married, your former spouse would not learn your current address from the tribunal process. It is true that both parties to a marriage have a right to give evidence about it if they choose to do that even if one is said to have been abusive. Your family members can be witnesses. The professionals who have been helping you recover from spousal and substance abuse would be excellent witnesses. I hope you will make the effort to present your case and truly put this past relationship behind you. *Sister Faith*

LEGITIMACY OF CHILDREN AFTER DECLARATION OF NULLITY

Q. HOW DOES THE CHURCH VIEW THE OFFSPRING OF Catholics who have had their marriage declared null? The parents of a friend divorced years ago. His mother sought and was granted a declaration of nullity from the Catholic Church. He has much heartache resulting from the perception that he is somehow illegitimate. Thanks, *Harry*

R. THE CHILDREN OF A MARRIAGE THAT HAS BEEN DECLARED null by the Catholic Church remain legitimate. Legitimacy flows from civil law. If a marriage lacked something essential that prevented it from being a union binding for life according to Church law, it is still a valid civil marriage, just not a valid canonical one. Children remain legitimate. *Sister Faith*

Scheduling the Next Wedding

Q. When can we schedule our wedding? My fiancée is divorced and currently applying for a declaration of nullity. She has not heard anything back yet from her parish church. Is it possible to schedule a date through the parish church even though she has not heard back yet or should she wait before we do anything? It is difficult to coordinate a reception and a church not knowing anything at this point. Thank you, *Scott*

R. It is my understanding that most dioceses and archdioceses have policies stating that ceremonies cannot be scheduled in Catholic churches until a declaration of nullity is received. That's the way it is in the diocese where I live. One reason for this is that not all marriages can be declared null. I would hope she will get the results sooner rather than later. She is allowed to contact the tribunal and request a status report on her case. May God bless you both. I'll pray for you. Peace, *Father Mike*

Length of Time a Case Takes

Q. How long does a marriage case take once the paperwork is completed? *Lori*

R. THE TIME IT TAKES TO PROCESS A MARRIAGE CASE VARIES depending on the difficulty of the case and the current caseload of the tribunal that is processing the case.

And, some cases are easier than others. For example, cases that are called "Lack of Form" cases might take a few days to a few weeks. A Formal case usually takes much longer. My experience is that a Formal case takes between twelve and eighteen months on average. Some are faster; some are slower. With Formal cases, witnesses are asked to offer testimony, and if the witnesses don't respond in a timely manner, the case is not completed quickly. *Father Mike*

Q. IS THERE ANYTHING WE CAN DO TO SPEED UP THE marriage case process since we are in a time of war and he will be leaving the country soon?

We were told that the Diocese of the Military is usually pretty fast but we have been working on this for over a year and it has been a slow process. His former wife did not respond to the process. She has remarried and has had a child already. She was the Catholic in the previous marriage but was never practicing to any extent. *Katherine*

R. THE ONLY THING YOUR INTENDED SPOUSE CAN DO IS respond immediately to any requests sent to him by the tribunal.

I am concerned about the pressure on both of you with this being a time of war. I cannot tell you the number of cases I have seen where a divorce has happened and one of

the spouses comes to the tribunal saying that he or she was
not thinking clearly at the time of the wedding but rushed
to marry before the other spouse went into a war situation.
The tribunal process is offering both of you time to be sure
of your decision to marry each other, a decision that should
only strengthen if you are separated by war. Please do not
rush into something that is to last for the rest of your lives.
It is too important to allow any pressure to influence your
serious evaluation of each other and your values. I hope one
of those values is to make a serious and considered
commitment for life not rushed by current pressures. You
are both in my prayers. *Sister Faith*

THE FINANCIAL COST

Q. CAN YOU GIVE A RANGE OF THE COSTS? *Al*

R. IT DEPENDS ON HOW THE INDIVIDUAL DIOCESE FINANCES
their Church court. In some places, each parish is assessed
an amount to pay for all the cases so there is no charge to an
individual parishioner.

In many places, the diocese picks up most of the
$1500–$2000 cost of processing a Formal case while the
petitioner is asked to pay a nominal fee of about $300. In
some dioceses, it has been decided that the petitioner
should pay most of the cost. You can find out the cost for
your diocese by asking at any parish. *Sister Faith*

Rejected Petition

Q. Does the Church ever say no to a marriage case? No offense but I don't understand how after many years of marriage anyone can say a marriage was invalid from the beginning. I have read all of these responses on a daily basis and my fiancée is going through the process now. I could be terribly wrong in saying this, but it appears that too many marriages are declared null. I just can't figure this out. *John*

R. A marriage case does not always receive an affirmative decision.

A negative decision means that as far as the experts at the tribunal can determine this was a valid marriage that one or both parties gave up on. The fact that your fiancée is presenting a case does not guarantee that she will ever be free to marry you.

Unfortunately, in the United States, there are many situations of invalid marriage for a variety of reasons. Many people do not regard marriage as a lifetime commitment about which they should take time to discern with great care, evaluating themselves and each other as potential spouses. There are also psychological illnesses that can prevent a valid commitment. It is really impossible to judge the marriage of someone you only know "from the outside," which leaves us needing to trust the expertise of tribunal officials as they apply Church law to a specific marriage. Sometimes a couple realizes the marriage is not a valid one soon after the wedding but they stay in a troubled relationship for many years until the child (sometimes the reason for the wedding in the first place with pregnancy before marriage) is old enough to understand the divorce. I hope this helps you understand the process. *Sister Faith*

Q. WHY HAVE I BEEN DENIED? WHY SHOULD I HAVE TO suffer? I have been denied a declaration of nullity by the tribunal. My ex-wife left me for no other reason than she found another man. I tried to get my marriage declared null and I have been denied. Now, should I ever choose to remarry, I cannot marry in the Catholic Church. I have done nothing wrong in this case whatsoever. I was a loving, caring husband. I am questioning my faith. I cannot believe this has just happened to me. The reason I was not granted the declaration of nullity was because abandonment is not considered a reason for nullity. My parish priest was trying to pull out of me other possible reasons as to why I should be granted one. Was it that she did not want to have children? No, we have three. Was it because she was an alcoholic? No, she was a healthy athlete. Why would I try to lie and make something up about my previous marriage when all I did was get divorce papers thrown in front of me? I don't get it. *John*

R. I AM GLAD YOU TOLD THE TRUTH IN THE INFORMATION THAT you presented to the tribunal.

When I am working with someone in the early stages of a case, I try to share with them that all cases presented to a marriage tribunal do not result in declarations of nullity. In order for a marriage to be declared invalid by the Catholic

Church, something essential to marriage, as defined by the Church, has to be missing at the time of consent. Things that happen after the wedding day that lead to the break up of the marriage cannot, on their own, be grounds for a declaration of nullity. However, the events after the wedding day may point to something that was missing at the time of consent. That's the reason why your parish priest was trying to "pull" other reasons out of you.

For example, being unhappy in the marriage and getting divorced is not a ground for a declaration of nullity. But, an intention at the time of the wedding to leave the marriage if unhappiness should come may be a reason for a declaration of nullity. The civil law result is the same: the parties are divorced, and the marriage is over. But, in the second example, one of the parties has redefined marriage by intending to leave the marriage if they become unhappy. They have, in tribunal terms, an intention against permanence. They redefined the understanding of marriage, contradicting what the Catholic Church teaches marriage to be, and they carried their definition with them at the time of the wedding. *Father Mike*

APPEAL PROCESS

Q. WHY DOES AN INVALID MARRIAGE DECLARATION NEED A "second opinion" or an appeal? I married a non-Catholic who was divorced. We are undergoing the tribunal process right now. We have received word that our diocese has found his previous marriage invalid but now are waiting for a second opinion. *Cindy*

R. THE SECOND OPINION ABOUT WHICH YOU SPEAK IS A
requirement that all affirmative decisions receive a
mandatory review by a court of second instance. Normally,
the process takes less time since all the material is already
gathered. This is but one case among hundreds being heard
in a tribunal. *Father Francis*

Q. IF A RESPONDENT APPEALS AN AFFIRMATIVE DECISION TO
the Roman Rota, how likely is it that Rome would accept the
appeal and how long would the entire process take to come
to conclusion? *Alice*

R. I don't have any firm answers for you. I would
presume that it would be very likely that the Roman Rota
would accept the appeal. Cases that go to the ordinary
appeal court take an average of two to three months. Cases
that go to the Roman Rota (the Roman Rota is the
extraordinary appeal court) take much longer. I've never
seen a published average length of time on cases appealed
to the Roman Rota. Peace, *Father Mike*

PART 4:

CONCLUSION

I would like to end this book with a story about grace and the Sacrament of Matrimony. You may know some people who have lived out their marital commitment for life. We need to celebrate those faithful spouses. Some people will say they do not want to call attention to themselves by celebrating twenty-five, forty or fifty years of marriage. I like to remind these couples that they owe it to the younger people in their parish to model that marriage is more than a wedding day and does not necessarily end in divorce. Moreover, marriage is meant to be for life.

In some marriage relationships there are details that could be an indication of possible reasons for invalidity. Those who marry under the pressures of war time, those who date briefly, those who come from different ethnic backgrounds or cultures, those who begin marriage with enforced separation, those who marry very young, those who wed with a significant age gap between the spouses as well as those who may marry without sufficient time to know each other well enough or to meet and know the family of the intended spouse—all have serious issues that could indicate invalidity. After I teach those who are preparing to help present marriage cases for their parishes about some of these red flags to note in listening to a person's history, I also tell them that marriages with seemingly a multitude of "red flags" can, through love, commitment and God's grace, endure. To explain what I mean, I use the example of my parents' marriage.

My mother was a convert to Catholicism. Working at a parachute factory in Australia during World War II, she walked past a Mercy convent each day and began talking with the Mother Superior who was often in the garden. My mother became increasingly interested in the Catholic faith, and ultimately these talks with the Mother Superior led to instructions in the faith and my mother's baptism as a Roman Catholic. Soon after that Mom asked about becoming a Sister of Mercy. The Mother Superior, a wise woman, told Mom that her desire to be a sister was most likely "first fervor of the faith," and if she still felt called in a few years she should come back to talk about a religious vocation. (Luckily for my four brothers and me God had other plans for Mom.)

Meanwhile, with the First Division of the United States Marines, my father invaded the Pacific Islands and was later sent with the other survivors of the battle to Australia to rest from war fatigue. At the time, Dad was also suffering from malaria, and under the influence of "tolerance level" quinine. During that time, Mom and Dad met and within six months they married. (If you have learned anything from reading this book, you might be thinking already there are red flags galore here: wartime, illness, lack of time for discernment, influence of medication, different backgrounds [Australia, United States] and faiths [cradle Catholic, convert] and a very brief courtship! It would seem to be a tribunal's dream case! But, wait; there is even more.)

On the wedding day, my nineteen-year-old mother proceeded down the aisle at the Church and she found no groom waiting for her at the altar. She and the rest of the wedding party presumed that my twenty-five-year-old father was probably ill with malaria and still in the sacristy. Mom and wedding party proceeded around the altar, and there, in the sacristy, on the floor, with a cold towel on his head, was Dad. They managed to move him to a bench. When the organ began to play the wedding march, the three-hundred-pound Jesuit priest who was sitting on the bench with Dad jumped up. The bench popped up and hit my Dad in the head and knocked him out. After Dad was revived and able to walk, they all proceeded out to the altar and my parents finally exchanged their marital vows.

Things are not always as they seem and neither are wedding days. What could have been the beginning of a disaster, turned out to be a fifty-four-year-long marriage that ended with my father's death in 1997. My parents' story proves that there is grace in the Sacrament of Matrimony and that just because something is likely to cause a marriage to fail does not mean it will do so. The opposite is also true: just because everything looks perfect on the wedding day, there is no guarantee this is a valid marriage.

This book has been put together from Web site responses to questions about marriage, divorce and the tribunal process. I hope it has offered you a painless way to learn about Catholic Church teaching as it relates to marriage.

Canons cited with permission from *Code of Canon Law,
Latin-English Edition, New English Translation*.
Washington: Canon Law Society of America, 1999.

For the complete list of canons and commentary on them
consult: *New Commentary on the Code of Canon Law*. Ed.
by John P. Beal, James A. Coriden and Thomas J. Green.
Mahwah, N.J.: Paulist Press, 2000, pp. 1234-1392, 1760-1768.

**Book IV: The Sanctifying Function of the Church, Part I: The
Sacraments, Title VII: Marriage
Canons 1055-1165**

**Foundational Canons
Canons 1055-1062**

Canon 1055

§1. The matrimonial covenant, by which a man and a
woman establish between themselves a partnership of
the whole of life and which is ordered by its nature to
the good of the spouses and the procreation and
education of offspring, has been raised by Christ the
Lord to the dignity of a sacrament between the baptized.

§2. For this reason, a valid matrimonial contract cannot exist
between the baptized without it being by that fact a
sacrament.

Canon 1056

The essential properties of marriage are unity and indissolubility, which in Christian marriage obtain a special firmness by reason of the sacrament.

Canon 1057

§1. The consent of the parties, legitimately manifested between persons qualified by law, makes marriage; no human power is able to supply this consent.

§2. Matrimonial consent is an act of the will by which a man and a woman mutually give and accept each other through an irrevocable covenant in order to establish marriage.

Canon 1058

All persons who are not prohibited by law can contract marriage.

Canon 1059

Even if only one party is Catholic, the marriage of Catholics is governed not only by divine law but also by canon law, without prejudice to the competence of civil authority concerning the merely civil effects of the same marriage.

Canon 1060

Marriage possesses the favor of law; therefore, in a case of doubt, the validity of a marriage must be upheld until the contrary is proven.

Canon 1061

§1. A valid marriage between the baptized is called ratum tantum if it has not been consummated; it is called ratum et consummatum if the spouses have performed between themselves in a human fashion a conjugal act which is suitable in itself for the procreation of offspring, to which marriage is ordered by its nature and by which the spouses become one flesh.

§2. After a marriage has been celebrated, if the spouses have lived together consummation is presumed until the contrary is proven.

§3. An invalid marriage is called putative if at least one party celebrated it in good faith, until both parties become certain of its nullity.

Canon 1062

§1. A promise of marriage, whether unilateral or bilateral, which is called an engagement, is governed by the particular law established by the conference of bishops, after it has considered any existing customs and civil laws.

§2. A promise to marry does not give rise to an action to seek the celebration of marriage; an action to repair damages, however, does arise if warranted.

Chapter I: Pastoral Care and Those Things Which Must Precede the Celebration of Marriage
Canons 1063–1072

Canon 1063
Pastors of souls are obliged to take care that their ecclesiastical community offers the Christian faithful the assistance by which the matrimonial state is preserved in a Christian spirit and advances in perfection. This assistance must be offered especially by:

preaching, catechesis adapted to minors, youth, and adults, and even the use of instruments of social

communication, by which the Christian faithful are
instructed about the meaning of Christian marriage and
about the function of Christian spouses and parents;
personal preparation to enter marriage, which disposes
the spouses to the holiness and duties of their new
state; a fruitful liturgical celebration of marriage which is
to show that the spouses signify and share in the
mystery of the unity and fruitful love between Christ
and the Church; help offered to those who are married,
so that faithfully preserving and protecting the conjugal
covenant, they daily come to lead holier and fuller lives
in their family.

Canon 1064

It is for the local ordinary to take care that such assistance is
organized fittingly, after he has also heard men and women
proven by experience and expertise if it seems opportune.

Canon 1065

§1. Catholics who have not yet received the sacrament of
confirmation are to receive it before they are admitted to
marriage if it can be done without grave inconvenience.

§2. To receive the sacrament of marriage fruitfully, spouses
are urged especially to approach the sacraments of
penance and of the Most Holy Eucharist.

Canon 1066

Before a marriage is celebrated, it must be evident that
nothing stands in the way of its valid and licit celebration.

Canon 1067

The conference of bishops is to establish norms about the
examination of spouses and about the marriage banns or
other opportune means to accomplish the investigations

necessary before marriage. After these norms have been diligently observed, the pastor can proceed to assist at the marriage.

Canon 1068
In danger of death and if other proofs cannot be obtained, the affirmation of the contracting parties, even sworn if the case warrants it, that they are baptized and are prevented by no impediment is sufficient unless there are indications to the contrary.

Canon 1069
All the faithful are obliged to reveal any impediments they know about to the pastor or local ordinary before the celebration of the marriage.

Canon 1070
If someone other than the pastor who is to assist at marriage has conducted the investigations, the person is to notify the pastor about the results as soon as possible through an authentic document.

Canon 1071
§1. Except in a case of necessity, a person is not to assist without the permission of the local ordinary at:
a marriage of transients; a marriage which cannot be recognized or celebrated according to the norm of civil law; a marriage of a person who is bound by natural obligations toward another party or children arising from a previous union; a marriage of a person who has notoriously rejected the Catholic faith; a marriage of a person who is under a censure; a marriage of a minor child when the parents are unaware or reasonably

opposed; a marriage to be entered into through a proxy as mentioned in canon 1105.

§2. The local ordinary is not to grant permission to assist at the marriage of a person who has notoriously rejected the Catholic faith unless the norms mentioned in canon 1125 have been observed with necessary adaptation.

Canon 1072
Pastors of souls are to take care to dissuade youth from the celebration of marriage before the age at which a person usually enters marriage according to the accepted practices of the region.

Chapter II: Diriment Impediments in General
Canons 1073-1082

Basic Principles

Canon 1073
A diriment impediment renders a person unqualified to contract marriage validly.

Canon 1074
An impediment which can be proven in the external forum is considered to be public; otherwise it is occult.

Canon 1075
§1. It is only for the supreme authority of the Church to declare authentically when divine law prohibits or nullifies marriage.

§2. Only the supreme authority has the right to establish other impediments for the baptized.

Canon 1076

A custom which introduces a new impediment or is contrary to existing impediments is reprobated.

Canon 1077

§1. In a special case, the local ordinary can prohibit marriage for his own subjects residing anywhere and for all actually present in his own territory but only for a time, for a grave cause, and for as long as the cause continues.

§2. Only the supreme authority of the Church can add a nullifying clause to a prohibition.

Dispensation from Impediments

Canon 1078

§1. The local ordinary can dispense his own subjects residing anywhere and all actually present in his own territory from all impediments of ecclesiastical law except those whose dispensation is reserved to the Apostolic See.

§2. Impediments whose dispensation is reserved to the Apostolic See are:

the impediment arising from sacred orders or from a public perpetual vow of chastity in a religious institute of pontifical right;

the impediment of crime mentioned in canon 1090.

§3. A dispensation is never given from the impediment of consanguinity in the direct line or in the second degree of the collateral line.

Canon 1079

§1. In urgent danger of death, the local ordinary can dispense his own subjects residing anywhere and all actually present in his territory both from the form to be observed in the celebration of marriage and from each and every impediment of ecclesiastical law, whether public or occult, except the impediment arising from the sacred order of presbyterate.

§2. In the same circumstances mentioned in §1, but only for cases in which the local ordinary cannot be reached, the pastor, the properly delegated sacred minister, and the priest or deacon who assists at marriage according to the norm of canon 1116, §2 possess the same power of dispensing.

§3. In danger of death a confessor possesses the power of dispensing from occult impediments for the internal forum, whether within or outside the act of sacramental confession.

§4. In the case mentioned in §2, the local ordinary is not considered accessible if he can be reached only through telegraph or telephone.

Canon 1080

§1. Whenever an impediment is discovered after everything has already been prepared for the wedding, and the marriage cannot be delayed without probable danger of grave harm until a dispensation is obtained from the competent authority, the local ordinary and, provided that the case is occult, all those mentioned in canon 1079, §§2-3 when the conditions prescribed therein have been observed possess the power of dispensing from all impediments except those mentioned in canon 1078, §2, n. 1.

§2. This power is valid even to convalidate a marriage if there is the same danger in delay and there is insufficient time to make recourse to the Apostolic See or to the local ordinary concerning impediments from which he is able to dispense.

Canon 1081

The pastor or the priest or deacon mentioned in canon 1079, §2 is to notify the local ordinary immediately about a dispensation granted for the external forum; it is also to be noted in the marriage register.

Canon 1082

Unless a rescript of the Penitentiary provides otherwise, a dispensation from an occult impediment granted in the non-sacramental internal forum is to be noted in a book which must be kept in the secret archive of the curia; no other dispensation for the external forum is necessary if afterwards the occult impediment becomes public.

Chapter III: Diriment Impediments Specifically
Canons 1083–1094

Canon 1083

§1. A man before he has completed his sixteenth year of age and a woman before she has completed her fourteenth year of age cannot enter into a valid marriage.

§2. The conference of bishops is free to establish a higher age for the licit celebration of marriage.

Canon 1084

§1. Antecedent and perpetual impotence to have intercourse, whether on the part of the man or the woman, whether absolute or relative, nullifies marriage by its very nature.

§2. If the impediment of impotence is doubtful, whether by a doubt about the law or a doubt about a fact, a marriage must not be impeded nor, while the doubt remains, declared null.

§3. Sterility neither prohibits nor nullifies marriage, without prejudice to the prescript of canon 1098.

Canon 1085

§1. A person bound by the bond of a prior marriage, even if it was not consummated, invalidly attempts marriage.

§2. Even if the prior marriage is invalid or dissolved for any reason, it is not on that account permitted to contract another before the nullity or dissolution of the prior marriage is established legitimately and certainly.

Canon 1086

§1. A marriage between two persons, one of whom has been baptized in the Catholic Church or received into it and has not defected from it by a formal act and the other of whom is not baptized, is invalid.

§2. A person is not to be dispensed from this impediment unless the conditions mentioned incanons 1125 and 1126 have been fulfilled.

§3. If at the time the marriage was contracted one party was commonly held to have been baptized or the baptism was doubtful, the validity of the marriage must be presumed according to the norm of canon 1060 until it is proven with certainty that one party was baptized but the other was not.

Canon 1087

Those in sacred orders invalidly attempt marriage.

Canon 1088

Those bound by a public perpetual vow of chastity in a religious institute invalidly attempt marriage.

Canon 1089

No marriage can exist between a man and a woman who has been abducted or at least detained with a view of contracting marriage with her unless the woman chooses marriage of her own accord after she has been separated from the captor and established in a safe and free place.

Canon 1090

§1. Anyone who with a view to entering marriage with a certain person has brought about the death of that person's spouse or of one's own spouse invalidly attempts this marriage.

§2. Those who have brought about the death of a spouse by mutual physical or moral cooperation also invalidly attempt a marriage together.

Canon 1091

§1. In the direct line of consanguinity marriage is invalid between all ancestors and descendants, both legitimate and natural.

§2. In the collateral line marriage is invalid up to and including the fourth degree.

§3. The impediment of consanguinity is not multiplied.

§4 A marriage is never permitted if doubt exists whether the partners are related by consanguinity in any degree of the direct line or in the second degree of the collateral line.

Canon 1092

Affinity in the direct line in any degree invalidates a marriage.

Canon 1093

The impediment of public propriety arises from an invalid marriage after the establishment of common life or from notorious or public concubinage. It nullifies marriage in the first degree of the direct line between the man and the blood relatives of the woman, and vice versa.

Canon 1094

Those who are related in the direct line or in the second degree of the collateral line by a legal relationship arising from adoption cannot contract marriage together validly.

Chapter IV: Matrimonial Consent
Canons 1095–1107

Canon 1095

The following are incapable of contracting marriage:
those who lack the sufficient use of reason;
those who suffer from a grave defect of discretion of judgment concerning the essential matrimonial rights and duties mutually to be handed over and accepted;
those who are not able to assume the essential obligations of marriage for causes of a psychic nature.

Canon 1096

§1. For matrimonial consent to exist, the contracting parties must be at least not ignorant that marriage is a permanent partnership between a man and a woman ordered to the procreation of offspring by means of some sexual cooperation.

§2. This ignorance is not presumed after puberty.

Canon 1097

§1. Error concerning the person renders a marriage invalid.

§2. Error concerning a quality of the person does not render a marriage invalid even if it is the cause for the contract, unless this quality is directly and principally intended.

Canon 1098

A person contracts invalidly who enters into a marriage deceived by malice, perpetrated to obtain consent, concerning some quality of the other partner which by its very nature can gravely disturb the partnership of conjugal life.

Canon 1099

Error concerning the unity or indissolubility or sacramental dignity of marriage does not vitiate matrimonial consent provided that it does not determine the will.

Canon 1100

The knowledge or opinion of the nullity of a marriage does not necessarily exclude matrimonial consent.

Canon 1101

§1. The internal consent of the mind is presumed to conform to the words and signs used in celebrating the marriage.

§2. If, however, either or both of the parties by a positive act of the will exclude marriage itself, some essential element of marriage, or some essential property of marriage, the party contracts invalidly.

Canon 1102

§1. A marriage subject to a condition about the future cannot be contracted validly.

§2. A marriage entered into subject to a condition about the past or the present is valid or not insofar as that which is subject to the condition exists or not.

§3. The condition mentioned in §2, however, cannot be placed licitly without the written permission of the local ordinary.

Canon 1103

A marriage is invalid if entered into because of force or grave fear from without, even if unintentionally inflicted, so that a person is compelled to choose marriage in order to be free from it.

Canon 1104

§1. To contract a marriage validly the contracting parties must be present together, either in person or by proxy.

§2. Those being married are to express matrimonial consent in words or, if they cannot speak, through equivalent signs.

Canon 1105

§1. To enter into a marriage validly by proxy it is required that: there is a special mandate to contract with a specific person; the proxy is designated by the one mandating and fulfills this function personally.

§2. To be valid the mandate must be signed by the one mandating and by the pastor or ordinary of the place where the mandate is given, or by a priest delegated by either of them, or at least by two witnesses, or it must be made by means of a document which is authentic according to the norm of civil law.

§3. If the one mandating cannot write, this is to be noted in the mandate itself and another witness is to be added who also signs the document; otherwise, the mandate is invalid.

§4. If the one mandating revokes the mandate or develops amentia before the proxy contracts in his or her name, the marriage is invalid even if the proxy or the other contracting party does not know this.

Canon 1106

A marriage can be contracted through an interpreter; the pastor is not to assist at it, however, unless he is certain of the trustworthiness of the interpreter.

Canon 1107

Even if a marriage was entered into invalidly by reason of an impediment or a defect of form, the consent given is presumed to persist until its revocation is established.

Chapter V: The Form of the Celebration of Marriage
Canons 1108–1123

The Elements of Canonical Form

Canon 1108

§1. Only those marriages are valid which are contracted before the local ordinary, pastor, or a priest or deacon delegated by either of them, who assist, and before two witnesses according to the rules expressed in the following canons and without prejudice to the exceptions mentioned in canons 144, 1112, §1, 1116, and 1127, §§1-2.

§2. The person who assists at a marriage is understood to be only that person who is present, asks for the manifestation of the consent of the contracting parties, and receives it in the name of the Church.

Requisites for Valid Assistance at Marriage

Canon 1109

Unless the local ordinary and pastor have been excommunicated, interdicted, or suspended from office or declared such through a sentence or decree, by virtue of their office and within the confines of their territory they assist validly at the marriages not only of their subjects but also of those who are not their subjects provided that one of them is of the Latin rite.

Canon 1110

By virtue of office, a personal ordinary and a personal pastor assist validly only at marriages where at least one of the parties is a subject within the confines of their jurisdiction.

Canon 1111

§1. As long as they hold office validly, the local ordinary and the pastor can delegate to priests and deacons the faculty, even a general one, of assisting at marriages within the limits of their territory.

§2. To be valid, the delegation of the faculty to assist at marriages must be given to specific persons expressly. If it concerns special delegation, it must be given for a specific marriage; if it concerns general delegation, it must be given in writing.

Canon 1112

§1. Where there is a lack of priests and deacons, the diocesan bishop can delegate lay persons to assist at marriages, with the previous favorable vote of the conference of bishops and after he has obtained the permission of the Holy See.

§2. A suitable lay person is to be selected, who is capable of giving instruction to those preparing to be married and able to perform the matrimonial liturgy properly.

Requirements for Licit Assistance at Marriages

Canon 1113

Before special delegation is granted, all those things which the law has established to prove free status are to be fulfilled.

Canon 1114

The person assisting at marriage acts illicitly unless the person has made certain of the free status of the contracting parties according to the norm of law and, if possible, of the permission of the pastor whenever the person assists in virtue of general delegation.

Canon 1115

Marriages are to be celebrated in a parish where either of the contracting parties has a domicile, quasi-domicile, or month-long residence or, if it concerns transients, in the parish where they actually reside. With the permission of the proper ordinary or proper pastor, marriages can be celebrated elsewhere.

The Extraordinary Canonical Form

Canon 1116

§1. If a person competent to assist according to the norm of law cannot be present or approached without grave inconvenience, those who intend to enter into a true marriage can contract it validly and licitly before witnesses only in danger of death;outside the danger of death provided that it is prudently foreseen that the situation will continue for a month.

§2. In either case, if some other priest or deacon who can be present is available, he must be called and be present at the celebration of the marriage together with the witnesses, without prejudice to the validity of the marriage before witnesses only.

Those Bound by the Canonical Form of Marriage

Canon 1117
The form established above must be observed if at least one of the parties contracting marriage was baptized in the Catholic Church or received into it and has not defected from it by a formal act, without prejudice to the prescripts of canon 1127, §2.

The Place Where Marriage Is to Be Celebrated

Canon 1118
§1. A marriage between Catholics or between a Catholic party and a non-Catholic baptized party is to be celebrated in a parish church. It can be celebrated in another church or oratory with the permission of the local ordinary or pastor.

§2. The local ordinary can permit a marriage to be celebrated in another suitable place.

§3. A marriage between a Catholic party and a non-baptized party can be celebrated in a church or in another suitable place.

The Liturgical Form of Marriage

Canon 1119
Outside the case of necessity, the rites prescribed in the liturgical books approved by the Church or received by legitimate customs are to be observed in the celebration of a marriage.

Canon 1120

The conference of bishops can produce its own rite of
marriage, to be reviewed by the Holy See, in keeping with
the usages of places and peoples which are adapted to the
Christian spirit; nevertheless, the law remains in effect that
the person who assists at the marriage is present, asks for
the manifestation of consent of the contracting parties, and
receives it.

The Recording of Marriages

Canon 1121

§1. After a marriage has been celebrated, the pastor of the
place of the celebration or the person who takes his
place, even if neither assisted at the marriage, is to note
as soon as possible in the marriage register the names of
the spouses, the person who assisted, and the witnesses,
and the place and date of the celebration of the
marriage according to the method prescribed by the
conference of bishops or the diocesan bishop.

§2. Whenever a marriage is contracted according to the
norm of canon 1116, a priest or deacon, if he was
present at the celebration, or otherwise the witnesses in
solidum with the contracting parties are bound to
inform as soon as possible the pastor or local ordinary
about the marriage entered into.

§3. For a marriage contracted with a dispensation from
canonical form, the local ordinary who granted the
dispensation is to take care that the dispensation and
celebration are inscribed in the marriage registers of
both the curia and the proper parish of the Catholic

party whose pastor conducted the investigation about the free status. The Catholic spouse is bound to notify as soon as possible the same ordinary and pastor about the marriage celebrated and also to indicate the place of the celebration and the public form observed.

Canon 1122

§1. The contracted marriage is to be noted also in the baptismal registers in which the baptism of the spouses has been recorded.

§2. If a spouse did not contract marriage in the parish in which the person was baptized, the pastor of the place of the celebration is to send notice of the marriage which has been entered into as soon as possible to the pastor of the place of the conferral of baptism.

Canon 1123

Whenever a marriage is either convalidated in the external forum, declared null, or legitimately dissolved other than by death, the pastor of the place of the celebration of the marriage must be informed so that a notation is properly made in the marriage and baptismal registers.

Chapter VI: Mixed Marriages
Canons 1124–1129

Canon 1124

Without express permission of the competent authority, a marriage is prohibited between two baptized persons of whom one is baptized in the Catholic Church or received into it after baptism and has not defected from it by a formal act and the other of whom is enrolled in a Church or ecclesial community not in full communion with the Catholic Church.

Canon 1125

The local ordinary can grant a permission of this kind if there is a just and reasonable cause. He is not to grant it unless the following conditions have been fulfilled:

§1. The Catholic party is to declare that he or she is prepared to remove dangers of defecting from the faith and is to make a sincere promise to do all in his or her power so that all offspring are baptized and brought up in the Catholic Church;

§2. The other party is to be informed at an appropriate time about the promises which the Catholic party is to make, in such a way that it is certain that he or she is truly aware of the promise and obligation of the Catholic party;

§3. Both parties are to be instructed about the purposes and essential properties of marriage which neither of the contracting parties is to exclude.

Canon 1126

It is for the conference of bishops to establish the method in which these declarations and promises, which are always required, must be made and to define the manner in which they are to be established in the external forum and the non-Catholic party informed about them.

Canon 1127

§1. The prescripts of canon 1108 are to be observed for the form to be used in a mixed marriage. Nevertheless, if a

Catholic party contracts marriage with a non-Catholic party of an Eastern rite, the canonical form of the celebration must be observed for liceity only; for validity, however, the presence of a sacred minister is required and the other requirements of law are to be observed.

§2. If grave difficulties hinder the observance of canonical form, the local ordinary of the Catholic party has the right of dispensing from the form in individual cases, after having consulted the ordinary of the place in which the marriage is celebrated and with some public form of celebration for validity. It is for the conference of bishops to establish norms by which the aforementioned dispensation is to be granted in a uniform manner.

§3. It is forbidden to have another religious celebration of the same marriage to give or renew matrimonial consent before or after the canonical celebration according to the norm of §1. Likewise, there is not to be a religious celebration in which the Catholic who is assisting and a non-Catholic minister together, using their own rites, ask for the consent of the parties.

Canon 1128

Local ordinaries and other pastors of souls are to take care that the Catholic spouse and the children born of a mixed marriage do not lack the spiritual help to fulfill their obligations and are to help spouses foster the unity of conjugal and family life.

Canon 1129

The prescripts of canons 1127 and 1128 must be applied also to marriages which the impediment of disparity of cult mentioned in canon 1086, §1 impedes.

Chapter VII: Marriage Celebrated Secretly
Canons 1130-1133

Canon 1130
For a grave and urgent cause, the local ordinary can permit a marriage to be celebrated secretly.

Canon 1131
Permission to celebrate a marriage secretly entails the following: the investigations which must be conducted before the marriage are done secretly; the local ordinary, the one assisting, the witnesses, and the spouses observe secrecy about the marriage celebrated.

Canon 1132
The obligation of observing the secrecy mentioned in canon 1131, n. 2 ceases on the part of the local ordinary if grave scandal or grave harm to the holiness of marriage is imminent due to the observance of the secret; this is to be made known to the parties before the celebration of the marriage.

Canon 1133
A marriage celebrated secretly is to be noted only in a special register to be kept in the secret archive of the curia.

Chapter VIII: The Effects of Marriage
Canons 1134-1140

Canon 1134
From a valid marriage there arises between the spouses a bond which by its nature is perpetual and exclusive. Moreover, a special sacrament strengthens and, as it were, consecrates the spouses in a Christian marriage for the duties and dignity of their state.

Canon 1135
Each spouse has an equal duty and right to those things which belong to the partnership of conjugal life.

Canon 1136
Parents have the most grave duty and the primary right to take care as best they can for the physical, social, cultural, moral, and religious education of their offspring.

Canon 1137
The children conceived or born of a valid or putative marriage are legitimate.

Canon 1138
§1. The father is he whom a lawful marriage indicates unless clear evidence proves the contrary.

§2. Children born at least 180 days after the day when the marriage was celebrated or within 300 days from the day of the dissolution of conjugal life are presumed to be legitimate.

Canon 1139

Illegitimate children are legitimated by the subsequent valid or putative marriage of their parents or by a rescript of the Holy See.

Canon 1140

As regards canonical effects, legitimated children are equal in all things to legitimate ones unless the law has expressly provided otherwise.

Chapter IX: The Separation of the Spouses
Canons 1141–1155

Article 1: Dissolution of the Bond
Canons 1141–1150

A. The Principle

Canon 1141

A marriage that is *ratum et consummatum* can be dissolved by no human power and by no cause, except death.

B. The Exceptions

1) Dissolution of a Ratified but Non-consummated Marriage

Canon 1142

For a just cause, the Roman Pontiff can dissolve a non-consummated marriage between baptized persons or between a baptized party and a non-baptized party at the request of both parties or of one of them, even if the other party is unwilling.

2) Dissolution by the Pauline Privilege

Canon 1143

§1. A marriage entered into by two non-baptized persons is dissolved by means of the pauline privilege in favor of the faith of the party who has received baptism by the very fact that a new marriage is contracted by the same party, provided that the non-baptized party departs.

§2. The non-baptized party is considered to depart if he or she does not wish to cohabit with the baptized party or to cohabit peacefully without affront to the Creator unless the baptized party, after baptism was received, has given the other a just cause for departing.

Canon 1144

§1. For the baptized party to contract a new marriage validly, the non-baptized party must always be interrogated whether: he or she also wishes to receive baptism; he or she at least wishes to cohabit peacefully with the baptized party without affront to the Creator.

§2. This interrogation must be done after baptism. For a grave cause, however, the local ordinary can permit the interrogation to be done before baptism or can even dispense from the interrogation either before or after baptism provided that it is evident at least by a summary and extrajudicial process that it cannot be done or would be useless.

Canon 1145

§1. The interrogation is regularly to be done on the authority of the local ordinary of the converted party. This ordinary must grant the other spouse a period of time to respond if the spouse seeks it, after having been advised, however, that his or her silence will be considered a negative response if the period passes without effect.

§2. Even an interrogation made privately by the converted party is valid and indeed licit if the form prescribed above cannot be observed.

§3. In either case, the fact that the interrogation was done and its outcome must be established legitimately in the external forum.

Canon 1146

The baptized party has the right to contract a new marriage with a Catholic party: if the other party responded negatively to the interrogation or if the interrogation had been omitted legitimately; if the non-baptized party, already interrogated or not, at first persevered in peaceful cohabitation without affront to the Creator but then departed without a just cause, without prejudice to the prescripts of canons 1144 and 1145.

Canon 1147

For a grave cause, however, the local ordinary can allow a baptized party who uses the pauline privilege to contract marriage with a non-Catholic party, whether baptized or not baptized; the prescripts of the canons about mixed marriages are also to be observed.

3) Dissolution in Virtue of Three Sixteenth Century Papal Constitutions

Canon 1148

§1. When he receives baptism in the Catholic Church, a non-baptized man who has several non-baptized wives at the same time can retain one of them after the others have been dismissed, if it is hard for him to remain with the first one. The same is valid for a non-baptized woman who has several non-baptized husbands at the same time.

§2. In the cases mentioned in §1, marriage must be contracted in legitimate form after baptism has been received, and the prescripts about mixed marriages, if necessary, and other matters required by the law are to be observed.

§3. Keeping in mind the moral, social, and economic conditions of places and of persons, the local ordinary is to take care that the needs of the first wife and the others dismissed are sufficiently provided for according to the norms of justice, Christian charity, and natural equity.

Canon 1149

A non-baptized person who, after having received baptism in the Catholic Church, cannot restore cohabitation with a non-baptized spouse by reason of captivity or persecution can contract another marriage even if the other party has received baptism in the meantime, without prejudice to the prescript of canon 1141.

4) Dissolution of a Non-sacramental Marriage "In Favor of the Faith"

Canon 1150

In a doubtful matter the privilege of faith possesses the favor of the law.

Article 2: Separation with the Bond Remaining
Canons 1151–1155

Canon 1151

Spouses have the duty and right to preserve conjugal living unless a legitimate cause excuses them.

Grounds for Separation

Canon 1152

§1. Although it is earnestly recommended that a spouse, moved by Christian charity and concerned for the good of the family, not refuse forgiveness to an adulterous partner and not disrupt conjugal life, nevertheless, if the spouse did not condone the fault of the other expressly or tacitly, the spouse has the right to sever conjugal living unless the spouse consented to the adultery, gave cause for it, or also committed adultery.

§2. Tacit condonation exists if the innocent spouse has had marital relations voluntarily with the other spouse after having become certain of the adultery. It is presumed, moreover, if the spouse observed conjugal living for six months and did not make recourse to the ecclesiastical or civil authority.

§3. If the innocent spouse has severed conjugal living voluntarily, the spouse is to introduce a cause for separation within six months to the competent ecclesiastical authority which, after having investigated all the circumstances, is to consider carefully whether the innocent spouse can be moved to forgive the fault and not to prolong the separation permanently.

Canon 1153

§1. If either of the spouses causes grave mental or physical danger to the other spouse or to the offspring or otherwise renders common life too difficult, that spouse gives the other a legitimate cause for leaving, either by decree of the local ordinary or even on his or her own authority if there is danger in delay.

§2. In all cases, when the cause for the separation ceases, conjugal living must be restored unless ecclesiastical authority has established otherwise.

Post-separation Issues

Canon 1154

After the separation of the spouses has taken place, the adequate support and education of the children must always be suitably provided.

Canon 1155

The innocent spouse laudably can readmit the other spouse to conjugal life; in this case the innocent spouse renounces the right to separate.

Chapter X: The Convalidation of Marriage
Canons 1156-1165

Article 1: Simple Convalidation
Canons 1156-1160

Canon 1156

§1. To convalidate a marriage which is invalid because of a diriment impediment, it is required that the impediment ceases or is dispensed and that at least the party conscious of the impediment renews consent.

§2. Ecclesiastical law requires this renewal for the validity of the convalidation even if each party gave consent at the beginning and did not revoke it afterwards.

Canon 1157

The renewal of consent must be a new act of the will concerning a marriage which the renewing party knows or thinks was null from the beginning.

Canon 1158

§1. The impediment is public, both parties must renew the consent in canonical form, without prejudice to the prescript of canon 1127, §2.

§2. If the impediment cannot be proven, it is sufficient that the party conscious of the impediment renews the consent privately and in secret, provided that the other perseveres in the consent offered; if the impediment is known to both parties, both are to renew the consent.

Canon 1159

§1. A marriage which is invalid because of a defect of consent is convalidated if the party who did not consent now consents, provided that the consent given by the other party perseveres.

§2. If the defect of consent cannot be proven, it is sufficient that the party who did not consent gives consent privately and in secret.

§3. If the defect of consent can be proven, the consent must be given in canonical form.

Canon 1160

A marriage which is null because of defect of form must be contracted anew in canonical form in order to become valid, without prejudice to the prescript of canon 1127, §2.

Article 2: Radical Sanation
Canons 1161-1165

Canon 1161

§1. The radical sanation of an invalid marriage is its convalidation without the renewal of consent, which is granted by competent authority and entails the dispensation from an impediment, if there is one, and from canonical form, if it was not observed, and the retroactivity of canonical effects.

§2. Convalidation occurs at the moment of the granting of the favor. Retroactivity, however, is understood to extend to the moment of the celebration of the marriage unless other provision is expressly made.

§3. A radical sanation is not to be granted unless it is probable that the parties wish to persevere in conjugal life.

Radical Sanation in Various Circumstances

1. Sanation and Defective Consent

Canon 1162

§1. A marriage cannot be radically sanated if consent is lacking in either or both of the parties, whether the consent was lacking from the beginning or, though present in the beginning, was revoked afterwards.

§2. If this consent was indeed lacking from the beginning but was given afterwards, the sanation can be granted from the moment the consent was given.

2. Sanation and Impediments or Defect of Form

Canon 1163

§1. A marriage which is invalid because of an impediment or a defect of legitimate form can be sanated provided that the consent of each party perseveres.

§2. A marriage which is invalid because of an impediment of natural law or of divine positive law can be sanated only after the impediment has ceased.

3. Sanation without the Awareness of the Parties

Canon 1164

A sanation can be granted validly even if either or both of the parties do not know of it; nevertheless, it is not to be granted except for a grave cause.

Canon 1165

§1. The Apostolic See can grant a radical sanation.

§2. The diocesan bishop can grant a radical sanation in individual cases even if there are several reasons for nullity in the same marriage, after the conditions mentioned in canon 1125 for the sanation of a mixed marriage have been fulfilled. He cannot grant one, however, if there is an impediment whose dispensation is reserved to the Apostolic See according to the norm of canon 1078, §2, or if it concerns an impediment of natural law or divine positive law which has now ceased.

Section II: The Oral Contentious Process
Part III: Certain Special Processes
Title I: Marriages Processes

Chapter I: Cases to Declare the Nullity of Marriage

Article 1: The Competent Forum
Canons 1671-1673

Canon 1671
Marriage cases of the baptized belong to the ecclesiastical judge by proper right.

Canon 1672
Cases concerning the merely civil effects of marriage belong to the civil magistrate unless particular law establishes that an ecclesiastical judge can investigate and decide these cases if they are done in an incidental or accessory manner.

Canon 1673
In cases concerning the nullity of marriage which are not reserved to the Apostolic See, the following are competent: the tribunal of the place in which the marriage was celebrated; the tribunal of the place in which the respondent has a domicile or quasi-domicile; the tribunal of the place in which the petitioner has a domicile, provided that both parties live in the territory of the same conference of bishops and the judicial vicar of the domicile of the respondent gives consent after he has heard the respondent; the tribunal of the place in which in fact most of the proofs must be collected, provided that consent is given by the judicial vicar of the domicile of the respondent, who is first to ask if the respondent has any exception to make.

Article 2: The Right to Challenge a Marriage
Canons 1674–1675

Canon 1674
The following are qualified to challenge a marriage:
the spouses; the promoter of justice when nullity has already
become public, if the convalidation of the marriage is not
possible or expedient.

Canon 1675
§1. A marriage which was not accused while both spouses
were living cannot be accused after the death of either
one or both of the spouses unless the question of
validity is prejudicial to the resolution of another
controversy either in the canonical forum or in the civil
forum.

§2. If a spouse dies while the case is pending, however,
canon 1518 is to be observed.

About the Author

Sister Victoria Vondenberger is a Sister of Mercy who has been involved in tribunal work for fourteen years. She is a presenter of workshops for the Canon Law Society of America and an author of *Procedural Handbook for Institute of Consecrated Life and Societies of Apostolic Life*, as well as several articles for *Jurist, Studia canonica* and *St. Anthony Messenger*. Sister Victoria was also one of four editors on the important canonical text, *Jurisprudence: A Collection of U.S. Tribunal Decisions*.

She received her *Juris canonici licentiate* degree in canon law in 1990 from St. Paul Pontifical University in Ottawa, Canada and a Master's degree in canon law from Ottawa University. She currently serves as Director of the Tribunal, Defender of the Bond and Promoter of Justice in Cincinnati. She also teaches canon law at The Athenaeum of Ohio. Through the Lay Pastoral Ministry Program, she also instructs lay men and women, deacons and religious to become procurator/advocates for the Archdiocese of Cincinnati. These adult students seek to become certified to help people present marriage cases to the tribunal. She has been recommending the OnceCatholic.org Web site to her students since she first became aware of it and has found their responses to the site to be very positive.

If your reading of these questions and responses raises further issues for you, please post your questions to the Web site: OnceCatholic.org in the Marriage Room. If you do not have Internet access, you may write to the author and she will post your question(s) for you and copy the response(s) to send them back to you.

Sister Victoria Vondenberger, R.S.M, J.C.L.
Tribunal Office
Archdiocese of Cincinnati
100 East 8th Street
Cincinnati, OH 45202